To Nancy & Ted

Best Wishes

Adeline Pardo

To Nancy + Paddy

LOOSE LEAD

The Life and Dog-Training Secrets
of Texas Legend Adelene Pardo

by

Nancy Francis

Nancy Francis

LOOSE LEAD: The Life and Dog-Training Secrets of Texas Legend Adelene Pardo
©2003 by Nancy Francis and Adelene Pardo

Illustrations by Jeanne Troxel

Manufactured in the United States of America.

ISBN: 0-9726822-0-1

Library of Congress Control Number: 2002116262

This book is available at quantity discounts for bulk purchases.

Brazos Valley Press
P.O. Box 215
Calvert, Texas 77837-0215
979.364.2439
www.brazosvalleypress.com

This book is dedicated to
Hector and Lena Cullum
Jim and Addie Lacina
Don Francis

Contents

Foreword

Venus was a beautiful, graceful, red-and-rust Doberman with penetrating brown eyes. Her master was my new husband, and the instant she and I met, early in 1990, I realized that all the popular myths about Dobermans were fiction. Venus was a great friend who guided me gently through my first experience as a "dog mom." She taught me many lessons, and we shared many adventures. Venus constantly amazed me with her intelligence and instincts. She never forgot a friend or the sound of a certain car, and she knew from my reaction whether someone was an acquaintance or unknown. "The V," as we called her, was an impeccable judge of character, and I trusted her implicitly.

She was always ready to go out, and we took long walks in the neighborhood until one day I realized she really wanted to run. And so an 11-year-old Doberman patiently taught a non-runner to run. As the years passed, we slowed to a jog, but we remained exercise buddies until three months after her 14th birthday, the day before what would have been our third annual "fun run" in downtown Houston. Suddenly, Venus was not feeling well. Congestive heart failure was the diagnosis; a month later she was gone. She grew old so gracefully it was hardly noticeable, and I was lost without her. I promised her I would continue to run, and on that first empty mile, the neighbors and their dogs told me they all missed Venus.

A couple of months later, I was on a mission to learn more about the breed that had given me so much. Through some pedigree research I traced Venus' ancestry to the great Ch. Dictator von Glenhugel, the most famous Doberman of the 1940s. Several books about Dobermans suggested that good puppies could be obtained through connections made at dog shows. With my husband, I attended the next local show, which happened to be part of the largest series of dog shows in the United States, known at the time as the Astrohall World Series of Dog Shows.

We had visited one of the shows at the Astrohall the year before and found ourselves surrounded by beautiful dogs and extremely knowledgeable owners and fanciers, who seemed to be speaking a foreign language. Entering the show grounds, we were immediately impressed by the number and variety of well-groomed, happy, handsome and well-behaved dogs, with their owners, handlers and various helpers busily making last-minute preparations. At that show, a woman we would later come to know as one of the top Doberman breeders in the country took the time to explain to us, a couple of strangers, how and why a dog show is conducted, the basic conformation judging procedure and some of the terminology. She pointed out certain dogs and noted their strengths and weaknesses. She never mentioned the considerable successes of her own dogs or dogs from her breeding program. And in that time she generously gave to strangers she met in the parking lot, she opened a door to the incredible world of dog shows. A couple of years later, a combination of extremely good luck, the support of good friends and an understanding husband enabled me to participate in that world.

My trip to the Astrohall in 1998 held special importance because I met several people who became friends, enabled me to find a very special puppy and guided me through the world of dog showing.

Our new puppy's breeders proved to be a valuable support team. They treated all the pups in the litter as their own and provided detailed information about puppy care. They welcomed us to their extended canine family and were cheerfully available to answer questions, share advice and provide whatever assistance we needed. To this day, they keep up with all their puppies.

I hoped to become involved in obedience competition, but my goofy red boy named Mars changed those plans. He would grow up to be more handsome than I ever imagined and lead me on an incredible journey.

We began working in obedience when he was four months old. Mars quickly earned the title "class clown." He taught me to play and laugh and forgive. At nine months, he had nearly reached his adult height and had continued to mature handsomely. His breeders and a few knowledgeable show friends encouraged me to show him in conformation. Generally speaking, a dog should be shown in conformation as a puppy and young adult; obedience competition can be undertaken when the dog is any age over six months. I welcomed the opportunity to be involved in conformation showing, especially since Mars was having a lot more fun in obedience than I.

Later, I would marvel at my luck to have acquired a show dog as a novice. I would meet many at the shows who claimed they couldn't find a good show prospect. When I set about searching for a good puppy, I never imagined finding a show-caliber dog. I was thrilled to have a well-bred dog and honored to have a show candidate.

I'll never forget the first time I pulled into an exhibitors' parking lot and saw row after row of motor homes, exercise pens, grooming tables, lawn chairs and barbecue grills. I had only begun to appreciate the mania of "show people."

One special friend, a retired professional all-breed handler, and her daughter, an expert groomer, taught me to how condition my puppy for the show ring. We groomed him together before the shows, and they would perform magic as they lectured on proper conditioning and the many other aspects of dog showing.

Another friend, a breeder and professional handler, handled Mars in the ring during the first few months of his show career. She expertly guided him to Reserve Winners Dog in his second show. Mars clearly enjoyed the show ring and displayed promise. After watching from outside the ring, I wanted to learn the art of handling so that I could present my own dog to the judges.

Learning to handle was an especially serious undertaking for me because competition in the Doberman ring in Texas is notoriously fierce. As a result, nearly all the handlers are professionals. Indeed, most of the Doberman show people must have doubted my sanity, for I was a rank novice whose instincts were to get into the ring and show my own dog. But one of the most valuable lessons I have learned from my dogs is to trust my instincts.

In search of a concentrated course, I attended a handling seminar and several different classes. I was also looking for a teacher of loose-lead handling because I liked the theory that my dog's correct structure and natural, easy movement would be emphasized on a loose lead. My quest turned up one person recommended by several diverse but knowledgeable sources: Adelene Pardo.

Mrs. Pardo watched Mars and me walk about 30 feet across the driveway prior to our first lesson and commented, "I like your dog, but I just don't think you're serious." During those first moments she had correctly determined that I thrive on challenge. The next several months were dedicated to proving to her, through hard work, that I was serious. During those first moments I determined that Mrs. Pardo is a wise and perceptive woman. I knew then that only a foolish person would come to her lessons unprepared, for not only would they be wasting money, they would lose the opportunity to learn from a master. That walk across the driveway was the beginning of many lessons and classes during which she taught me to show my dog with joy and pride. But Mrs. Pardo taught me a lot more than how to handle a dog; in the process, she made me realize many things about myself.

Mrs. Pardo has been involved in training and showing dogs for more than 40 years. As a licensed professional handler she "finished," or showed to championship, hundreds of dogs using the loose-lead style of handling. Today she teaches handling privately and in classes, gives seminars and is an active AKC Sporting Group judge. She travels to shows across the country and has also judged in international competitions.

Regarded by many in the dog show world as one of Texas' more colorful characters, Mrs. Pardo is highly respected and nationally known as a trainer and teacher of loose-lead handling. Her students, many of whom travel from other states for lessons, value her wealth of knowledge and experience, her honesty, her no-nonsense approach and her love of the sport and the animals.

One of Mrs. Pardo's former students, Anne Page, editor of *Canine Classified,* a monthly newsletter published in the Houston area, stated in a 1976 flyer advertising her classes that Adelene begins every training class with the statement, "There's a right way, a wrong way, and Adelene's way. In this class, we do it Adelene's way." She concluded that Adelene's students leave the class convinced that "Adelene's way must be the right way because it works." Ms. Page's statements are just as true today.

Working with Mrs. Pardo to prepare this book has been another of those incredible, insightful experiences on a par with learning to show my dog. She is a great lady, and I hope everyone enjoys her stories and teachings.

Nancy Francis
Texana's Travis v Royalmead, Ptd, CGC, TDIA ("Mars")
Lady Lexus V, CGC (Rescue) ("Andie")
Venus de River (1984–1998)

Adelene Cullum

His Bulldog puppy bucking and pitching, the young man opened the gate and pulled his charge into a conformation handling class. As soon as they had taken their places at the end of the line of several handlers and dogs, class began. The instructor asked them to move their dogs around an imaginary show ring. The young man had practiced with his pup every day since the last class, but moving him on a loose lead was still a dream. He followed the others around the imaginary ring, trying to maintain a modicum of control. The instructor asked the group to put their dogs in a show stance. She smiled at the young man and took the Bulldog's lead. The puppy gaited smoothly to the center of the group with the lead in a relaxed position. Talking softly to the dog, she placed in him a stack position in a few seconds. The young man watched in disbelief as his unruly puppy was transformed into a beautiful show dog. He had witnessed a demonstration of Adelene Pardo's "velvet hands."

M rs. Pardo was born with velvet hands, but her expertise in the art of loose-lead conformation handling is the result of hard work, a desire to be the best and a constant search for knowledge. She taught herself the loose-lead technique using library books, observation and practical experience. As a handler she was legendary. She began as a novice with a dog of questionable breeding and rose through the ranks of Texas' dog show world to become a licensed professional all-breed handler with her own kennel of champion Weimaraners.

Today she teaches loose-lead handling and judges dogs nationally and internationally. As a teacher she is a true master who combines an innate sense of psychology with a wealth of knowledge and an unwavering truthfulness. She continues her life-long quest for knowledge as a judge with an impeccable reputation and a great love for the sport of dog showing.

Adelene Cullum was born December 29, 1932, in Houston, Texas, to Hector and Lena Cullum. Her father was born in London, England, and immigrated to the United States at the age of four. Lena DeGeorge Cullum was born in Louisiana; her grandparents were from Italy. Adelene says she never tells anyone she's half English because no one would believe her. Her father was a short, heavy-set man who appeared to be Italian. She feels her talent for handling horses and dogs comes from the English side of her family, because her paternal grandmother's brother was said to be very good with animal training.

She was raised in a very poor family during the depression. Her father was ill during much of this time; they often had very little to eat. It was Adelene's job to care for her father while her mother worked. It was her responsibility to take him to the doctor three times a week. She says she never knew during the trips to the doctor whether her father would have an attack and pass out. After high school graduation, she went to work at Texaco Inc. as a keypunch operator. "You might say I graduated from the school of hard knocks," she says. She is grateful for her childhood because she learned quickly to use common sense, to work hard and to not think that life is a free ride.

Neighbors Jim and Addie Lacina had a horse and befriended Adelene and her family. Mr. Lacina taught her how to train and care for animals, especially horses. Adelene's nickname at that time was "Horsie." She says by now it must have changed to "Doggie." Mrs. Lacina and Adelene's mother taught her to cook and entertain; she doesn't remember not knowing how to cook. Her mother and Mrs. Lacina were special people for Adelene. "All children should have someone other than their parents from whom to learn," she says. Mr. Lacina was her hero; Mrs. Lacina was her angel.

In April 1953, a mutual friend introduced her to Lou Pardo at a roller rink where Lou was skating in competition. Lou proposed marriage to "the beautiful Italian" three days after they met; they were married a year later. She brought into the marriage an all-American dog, part Chow-Chow and part German Shepherd, that she had raised from a pup. He lived to be 14 years old.

After her mixed-breed dog died, Adelene took one of a neighbor's ailing Weimaraner puppy bitches. Her name was "Pardo's Blue Star," but they called her "Star." Adelene started training her in obedience and conformation, using library books and her horse-training knowledge. They named the puppy "Blue Star" because she had blue eyes as a puppy, although they changed to amber as she matured.

Another neighbor who showed Poodles encouraged Adelene to attend a Houston Kennel Club match in 1960. "I remember it like it was yesterday," she says. "Betty Moore was selling refreshments, and Norton Moore was helping set up the rings." Adelene and her Weimaraner pup won Best Puppy and Best of Breed in the regular class. She also won the Group competition in both classifications.

"That's when I got the bug," she laughs. "Every time I'd win, I cried. Bob Ditmar, who was ring steward, said, 'You're winning! Get back in there.' So he would tell me when to go back in the ring. He also told me how to dress properly." After such great success at her first show, Adelene took the ribbons to a frame shop and paid $12 to have them framed, "But that was like $100 now," she says. Star only lived eight more months after that first show. She died of hepatitis; Adelene was heart-broken.

The Pardos had many vet bills and no money to buy another pup, so Adelene made and sold aprons to buy her next Weimaraner bitch, "Duskin's Princess Shellie." Everyone called her "Duchess," and she became the foundation for their kennel, Weimar Castle. She finished the Utility Dog title and conformation championship at the same time. "I can remember running from one ring to the other, changing her collar as we ran," she says. Duchess was also a master in the field and water, working the birds.

The Pardos met Tony and Gabby Gwinner in 1962 on the Texas dog show circuit. Tony's motor home needed repair, and someone referred him to Lou, who was an expert mechanic. At that time, Tony and Gabby were showing a great Weimaraner called "Gwinner's Pinwheel." Adelene had been admiring Pinwheel from afar, and unknown to her, Gabby had been admiring Duchess in obedience. The broken motor home caused the two couples to become very close friends, or as Adelene says, "like family," and later, professional handling associates.

In 1966, with the help and guidance of the Gwinners, the Pardos bought the largest boarding kennel in Houston. Located in the Meyerland area of Houston, Adelene and her mother ran the kennel from 1966 to 1974.

Lou Pardo

Lou can work on motors and fix anything, so he became known among the dog show motor home travelers as a good repairman. At a show one year in West Texas, the great Poodle handler Bobby Peeples couldn't light the pilot light in his motor home, so he asked Lou to repair it. Lou was lying on the floor with his head under the cabinet trying to light that pilot light when the bathroom door opened and a beautiful girl came out. She had just taken a shower and was naked. She just stepped over Lou like he wasn't there and went up front to talk to Bobby. Then she came back, stepped over Lou again, and went back into the bathroom like nothing had happened.

Lou Pardo was born in Waco, Texas, on June 25, 1931. He was the middle child with an older brother and sister and a younger brother and sister. The Pardos lived on a small farm about five miles north of Waco with the usual farm animals and mixed-breed dogs. The only purebred dog Lou had seen in those days was a friend's Chow-Chow. Lou comments, "The reason for the farm was the large family that had to be supported on Dad's small salary." Lou's father worked for Lone Star Gas at that time and felt lucky to have a job during the depression.

Lou describes his life in Waco as "really uneventful . . . but that was typical of the times." The family remained there until Lou was 14, when his father's job moved to Hearne, 60 miles south of Waco. At first, Lou disliked the town, but Hearne became an exciting place for all the Pardos. Lou met twice as many friends as he had known in Waco, got to go hunting and fishing with his dad and went to work at the local airport, servicing planes and taking flying lessons.

Lou went into the U.S. Air Force just as the Korean War began and served until its conclusion. Discharged in July of 1952, and on his way back to Hearne, he says he made "one fatal mistake." He stopped in Houston to skate at one of the rinks, and there he met Adelene. He was into competitive roller skating, including men's freestyle, pairs, hockey and speed skating, and he won many awards.

One of Adelene's girlfriends introduced her to Lou, and he realized he could not possibly live without that "beautiful Italian." He proposed marriage on their third date, and in typical fashion Adelene informed him he would have to get a better job. At the time, he was just a lifeguard at the Gateway pool on South Main Street. Lou went to work for the Veterans Administration; they were married after a "proper waiting time" of one year. After a short time with the VA, Lou went to work for the U.S. Post Office, starting as a truck driver and retiring as a top investigator.

When Lou began making enough money, Adelene quit her job at Texaco and started her careers as a homemaker and professional handler. Lou became involved in showing dogs right along with Adelene, and soon he was handling in the ring in addition to repairing motor homes at the shows. He became a licensed AKC judge, although today he accepts very few assignments. In 1986, Lou retired from the U.S. government after 37 years of service. He came out of retirement to drive an oil tanker for a chemical company.

CH. DUSKIN'S PRINCESS SHELLIE, U.D.

"Duchess"

One year in San Antonio in an obedience competition, we were on the long sit and long down in Open, where you had to leave the ring. While we were out of the room, lightning struck the building. When we returned to the ring, all the dogs were gone except Duchess. She was sitting with her head cocked as if to ask, "What in the world is going on?" But she didn't leave like all the other dogs. She had not moved from the spot where I left her.

Many dog fanciers believe that everyone, during his life as a dog owner, has one particular dog that is closer to his heart than all the others. Some refer to this one special animal as their "heart dog." Adelene's most special dog was Ch. Duskin's Princess Shellie, U.D.

Adelene acquired Duchess after the death of her first Weimaraner. A dog-trainer friend who owned Weimaraners accompanied Adelene and Lou to the Montrose area of Houston to see her, and Adelene says, "She came bouncing out from behind the house. They had her chained to a tree, but her temperament and spirit were great." Adelene was a little worried because the puppy was five and a half months old and could have acquired some bad habits, but her friend advised, "You'll regret the day you don't buy this bitch." The price was $75, but Adelene only had $50 that she had earned from her apron enterprise. She gave the sellers the $50 and they held the papers. A neighbor who had Dobermans loaned her the remaining $25 until she could sell more aprons to repay the loan.

Adelene says that it was very easy to train Duchess because she "came to hand" so easily and always wanted to please. She taught Duchess the novice obedience exercises, including heel and sit,

sit-stay, down-stay, come-on-command, figure eight and stand-for-examination. "For practice we would go to food market parking lots and go through the obedience exercises. People would come in and out of the market while we were practicing and talk about her as they walked by. When Duchess did the stand-stay or the stand-for-examination, I would ask one of them to pat her on the head and down her neck and back. That's how she learned to stay. On the long sit and long down, I'd position her up against cars in a parking lot, in locations with cars going by her, in different temperatures and with dogs fighting at her through fences."

By the time Duchess was two years old, having been obedience trained, she went everywhere with the Pardos. "When we went to a restaurant we'd let down the tailgate, and she would lie in the station wagon on a little rug and wait for us while we ate," Adelene says. One time in a restaurant, a man tried to buy Duchess for his wife. Adelene told him Duchess wasn't for sale, but he laid a blank check on the table and asked Adelene to write the price on it. "Money can buy anything," he told her. Adelene informed him that all the money in Fort Knox would not be enough for Duchess, so he picked up the check and returned to his table. As Adelene and Lou were leaving, she asked the man how much money he would have paid for Duchess. "Six figures," he said. Adelene always thought that he had offered a hundred thousand dollars for Duchess.

"You could stake your life on her," she says. "You could do anything with her. Duchess was a good conformation dog, a good traveler, a good obedience dog and a real pal." Adelene continues, "When we used to go to New Orleans to the dog shows, we'd take her to the French Quarter and put her on a sit-stay outside the shops while we went in. She would sit and wait for us, and if anyone talked to her, she would turn her head away." They also took her to the Alamo. "Of course, they wouldn't let her into the Alamo, but we'd put her on a long sit-stay and go in. When we returned, she'd be waiting.

"Duchess always would lie on a rug at the shows. You could go off and leave her, and she would stay right there," Adelene says. Once while they were working for the Gwinners, Tony sent Adelene to a ring to show a dog while Lou was showing a dog in another ring. Adelene told Gabby to leave Duchess on the rug, that she would be fine and wouldn't go anywhere. After a while, Gabby told Adelene that she had put Duchess in a crate because she didn't want to go away and leave her. Duchess had never been in a crate, but because Gabby told her to get in the crate, she got in and waited quietly until they returned. Adelene continues, "Except for that one time, Duchess never stayed in a crate. She was just that well-trained. If you put a blanket down and told her to stay on it, she stayed there until you came back and got her. She was one hell of a dog!"

Duchess proved everyone but Adelene wrong during field exercises that were part of the weekly Weimaraner club activities. Formed during the 1960s, the Houston club would work on conformation and obedience one week; the next week they would do field work, like retrieving and pointing. Adelene remembers, "Duchess pointed a huge clump of weeds. One of the guys kicked the clump, but nothing came out. He kicked it again and again; still, nothing came out." The club members laughed and said that Duchess was wrong and that there wasn't a bird in the weeds.

The look in Duchess' eyes told Adelene there was a bird in the weeds. She told Lou he might have to cut them down one stem at a time because, "If Duchess says it's there, it's there, and I'm not calling her off this point." With much effort Lou was finally able to clear the weed clump and out came the bird. "And that just goes to show you need to trust your hunting dog. When she was as good as Duchess, you could bet your life on her."

Adelene continues, "She was a very special dog. I always said she even died on command. When she died in 1974, I was a licensed professional handler, so I had to go to a show with a load of dogs. I kissed her and asked her to hang on until I got back, and my Daddy stayed with her over the weekend. I came home on Monday and knelt down beside the couch, kissed her and told her, 'Let go, baby, I'm home,' and she died. She lived as she died, with great dignity."

Adelene recalls, "Duchess loved to ride the train. I used to take her to ride the train at Hermann Park in Houston. In San Antonio, we would ride a train that goes through a park. We got on at a station away from the main station. I bought an adult ticket for her; she would sit beside me, with her ears flapping in the breeze. As the train went past them, people just couldn't believe there was a dog sitting there, just like a human, enjoying the train ride. The weekend before she died, I took her to ride the train in Hermann Park."

Weimar Castle

My mother always prayed for me. I used to say to her as I was leaving for a show, "Momma, say a prayer for Thunderwheel so he'll win this weekend, and I'll send a donation to the church." Every weekend she would say a prayer for him, every weekend he would win and I would give her a donation for the church. After this went on for a long time, a letter came to the house addressed to Thunderwheel. It was from the head priest at Momma's church, thanking him for all the donations.

The Pardos chose Weimar Castle as their kennel name. One of Adelene's students designed a coat of arms for the logo featuring a Weimaraner. "W.C." is the abbreviation for Weimar Castle in the registered names of their dogs. Adelene showed several of her champion Weimaraners to placements in the national breed standings. Her first champion, of course, was Duchess, Ch. Duskin's Princess Shellie, U.D.

During their show careers, Ch. Gwinner's Telstarwheel ("Telstar"), Ch. W.C.'s Lancewheel ("Lancewheel") and Ch. W.C.'s Thunderwheel of Marquez, C.D. ("Thunderwheel") were each rated number three Weimaraner in the U.S. Telstar was a Breed and Group winner and was also in the top 10 Weimars in 1968.

W.C.'s The Dutchman of Dauntmar, BROM ("Dutchman") won three Best in Shows, was in the top 10 Weimaraners in the nation for 1973, 1974, 1975 and 1977 and won multiple Group competitions.

With Gabby Gwinner's encouragement, Adelene acquired the Dutchman as a pup from breeder Frank Sousa. Dauntmar was Frank Sousa's kennel name. The Dutchman was shipped to the Pardos. Lou met him at the airport and reported to Adelene that the Dutchman came out of the crate in a show stance. Adelene says the Dutchman was very easy to show and "perfect in conformation." She continues, "The only thing that beat him in the ring was when he gave it away, because he didn't like to show. Sometimes he was afraid, and we would lose if he acted up. If the Dutchman had Dago's temperament, I don't think anything could have beat him."

Adelene relates, "It was difficult to understand his temperament. Once when we were showing in Alexandria, we were on the edge of a tornado. The wind broke the skylight in the roof of the building and all the glass fell into the ring, but he wasn't one bit afraid. Then you could be somewhere quiet and a baby would cry and he would go to pieces. I just learned to listen to the noises and to be ready to grab him. I often wondered if he had been frightened when he flew on the plane coming to Texas. I think all dogs attach to the people who pick them up at the airport."

The Dutchman was also a special favorite of Adelene's father.

She continues, "Lancewheel, a puppy from Duchess and Thunderwheel, was a real big dog. Norton Moore finished him for me because I had just bought the boarding kennel and didn't have time to go to the shows. I showed him some as a special, but he had a really heavy coat that was not quite right for the Weimaraner standard.

Ch. W.C.'s Starwarwheel of Ranah ("Starwar") was the nation's number three Weimaraner in 1980, and a winner of Best in Show, specialties and Group competitions.

Ch. W.C.'s The Dynamic Dagowheel ("Dago") was one of the last great Weimaraners the Pardos showed. He was the number one Weimar in the nation in 1978 and 1979 and number one Weimar dog in 1980. In 1978 and 1979, Adelene campaigned Starwar and Dago as specials at the same time, entering one on one day and the other on the next day. Even though each dog only went to half the shows, both accumulated enough points to be rated in the top 10 Weimars in the country.

At first Adelene didn't quite comprehend Dago's beauty, as she realized when the Pardos took their motor home to one of Nolan River's earliest shows. Adelene was waiting at the Elkhound ring to show a couple of dogs. She looked out over the show grounds and spotted the most beautiful Weimaraner she had ever seen, gaiting across an open field near the motor home parking lot. She pointed him out to her friend, Cindy Victory Long, "Look at that gorgeous Weimaraner! I have to try to beat him today. There's no way! He's magnificent!"

As the beautiful dog approached them, Cindy laughed, "Adelene, that's Dago!" A few seconds later Lou walked over from the motor home, following Dago. It was routine at their motor home setup that Lou would open Dago's exercise pen, and he would run and jump into the motor home. On this particular day, when Dago looked in the door of the motor home and didn't see Adelene, he took a quick turn and came to the show rings to find her. "It was my own dog, and I didn't recognize him!" Adelene was not accustomed to seeing Dago gait from a distance because when they moved around the ring together, they were always side by side. Her view of him in the open field was very different. "That was the day I finally realized how absolutely magnificent he was." Dago came directly to Adelene and jumped around her, as if to announce "Well, I'm here. Let's go in the ring!"

Apparently the handsome Dago was also quite a "ladies' man." Adelene recalls, "At a specialty show in Dallas, we put his exercise pen outside in the grass. The Dallas Cowboys cheerleaders were performing at another event on the same grounds, and they came out to pet and hug him. Dago just loved women with perfume, and he leaned up against them and licked their faces with his little soft tongue. It was quite a scene. Everyone at the specialty, especially the men, came out with pooper-scoopers, pretending they were cleaning his pen, so they could get close to the Dallas Cowboys cheerleaders. Dago was something special with those cheerleaders."

She tells another story involving Dago and a wealthy client. "Sometimes she would bring her dog out in a Cadillac pickup truck, sometimes they'd bring him in the limousine. She always wore very expensive perfume. One time she came in the house and sat on the couch. Dago sat right in front of her, sniffing her perfume. She had on a real low-cut dress; he licked her right at the bottom of that low cut neckline. She looked at him and said 'Dago, if you were a man you'd make one hell of a lover!'"

During Dago's show career, when Adelene was bringing him to the ring, friends and admirers would clear a path for them, chanting "Here comes Dago; here comes Dago." Adelene would lay out a special red, white and blue rug for him at ringside; he would sit like a king, waiting his turn.

Thunderwheel was a replacement dog for a pup sired by Pinwheel, the Gwinners' stud dog. The puppy died of a condition that resulted from having had distemper. "Gabby told me that if I'd wait for Pinwheel's next breeding, she would give me a dog. That dog was Thunderwheel, from the Marquez kennels," Adelene states.

She continues, "Thunderwheel was a great dog. He was my little dog. He was just 25 inches tall, and every inch of him was a little toughie. He stood tall, walked smart, showed like a million bucks and was a bit of a fighter. He didn't fight at ringside or in the ring, but if a dog got tough with him in the kennel or yard next to him, he'd buck right up."

One of Adelene's friends wrote about Thunderwheel in a letter, "I don't suppose I shall ever forget that cocky little Thunderwheel. I guess he was proof to me that a little fellow can be a big man!"

Thunderwheel and Adelene traveled to the shows together frequently when Lou had to work. Adelene recalls, "We had this little jelly bean game we played. I'd lay a bag of jellybeans on the dashboard and try to get one out of the bag without Thunderwheel noticing. Somehow, he always knew." Thunderwheel would lie on the motor cover next to Adelene. "That's how I kept myself awake when I used to leave Little Rock, Arkansas, at 6 P.M. and drive all night to get home and open the kennel the next day."

Adelene continues, "Thunderwheel was a champion, and he also had a Companion Dog title, although I didn't work him much. I worked him in Open obedience, but after I started handling dogs and got my boarding kennel, I just didn't have time to go on with the rest of his obedience titles." She adds, "He was real good at retrieving water fowl. He loved that. He liked it better than pointing. At the time we had him, we also had Duchess. Duchess was so good at pointing birds, that we always used her and let Thunderwheel do the water work.

"One time when he was six months old, we went to Dallas to a field trial," she remembers. "Lou was letting the electric tailgate down on the station wagon, and Thunderwheel jumped down, took off for the water and was swimming around. He was six months old, waiting for us to get there and tell him to go get the birds. He truly did love it." She recalls that Thunderwheel's love name was "Sweet Sweet." "When you would say 'Sweet Sweet,' his little tail would just wag and he'd buck up. He was a showing machine. He loved to show. He loved to do everything. He was very full of life.

"Lou always had to stay away from the trials," notes Adelene, "because if the dogs saw him, they would go to him and start playing." Adelene was unaware that Lou had boarded the gunner's boat at one of the trials. In this type of trial, the examiners fire a gun from a boat, throw a dead bird into the water, and then the dog is sent to retrieve it. She continues, "The judge told me to send Thunderwheel. He was swimming toward the bird, looking like a million dollars. All at once, he stopped, smelled a little bit, turned to the left and swam over to Lou, who was in the boat. The judge said, 'Lady, I don't know who's in that boat, but he just cost you first place.' Lou thought about that for a while that day before he came back to land."

The Pardos had many obedience dogs who also worked well in the field. "I had one dog, Lancewheel, who worked well in the water," she says, "but he wanted no part of pointing birds. Weimaraners do that sometimes. They can do it all. They can point birds and retrieve ducks or birds out of the water. They'll hunt wild boar and deer in the counties where it's legal. But some of them just want to do one or the other. We've had some really good times," she reflects. "We were winners with the first dog we ever had, and I guess it never did stop. We've always worked very hard. We lost sometimes, and we've had a dog or two that wasn't the greatest in the world. But the majority of our dogs were in the top 10 Weimaraners at one time or another."

5

Adelene Pardo
Professional All-Breed Handler

> When Adelene went into the ring with a dog, it was kind of like the sea parting. Everyone just stood aside, and she walked through. When she handled your dog, she owned you, owned the dog and owned the place! People totally respected her and her handling ability. —CAROLYN WILLIS

The neighbor who taught her about horse training and general care of horses and animals, Jim Lacina, told Adelene when she was a child that she had velvet hands. When she took the reins or lead, the horse or dog would know what she wanted him to do, he said.

Another neighbor had a litter of unhealthy Weimaraners, and Adelene felt sorry for them. She took one, nursed it to health and trained it, using library books and her horse training knowledge. Yet another neighbor who showed Poodles encouraged Adelene to attend her first match on North Shepherd in Houston. Adelene says, "That's when it all got started. My Weimaraner won Best Sporting Puppy, and then she won Best in Show that night over the older dogs. That's when the bug hit."

She continued to study books from the library and watch other handlers at the shows. Adelene has a special memory of a Houston Kennel Club show at the city auditorium in downtown Houston. She went to the obedience ring to watch. She wrote notes in the back of a catalog about how the people walked, what they were wearing, how they held their leads and their attitudes. Then she went home and trained her bitch, Duchess. Later, she learned that the people she had been observing were students of the prominent

AKC judge and dog fancy personality Dorothy Nickles, "So I always say that Dorothy Nickles taught me obedience long-distance," she grins. At the time she didn't know Ms. Nickles; she just knew her students from watching them at the shows.

Throughout her career, Adelene continued to study other handlers in a constant effort to perfect her handling skills. "On the old Texas circuit, it would take one's breath away to see all the great dogs and great handlers. You could learn by just sitting, watching and listening to them," she states. After years of self-study and work, she became a licensed AKC all-breed professional handler, the ultimate recognition given a professional handler. Only the most competent achieved this classification, which is no longer in use.

Carolyn Willis, one of her former handling clients and a friend for 35 years, classifies Adelene as "the best handler I've ever seen." She continues, "It was an honor for her to handle your dog, because Adelene Pardo did not handle bad dogs. If someone asked her to handle a dog that was not good, she would tell them kindly to take their dog home and love him; he's not a show dog."

Ms. Willis says, "She'll never understand what a gift she is to the dog world. She is the essence of what a handler should be. She always puts the dog first. As a client, you knew that you bathed your dog and took it to her; then it was her dog. The dog understood that and the owners understood. They trusted her because she was the best." She adds, "Once she got her hands on them, the dogs fell in love with her. They were hers. Malamutes aren't known for liking other breeds, but mine loved the Weimars that were part of her life. He thought he was a Weimaraner.

"You didn't tell her anything about what to do," she continues. "It would be like trying to tell Picasso how to paint. You didn't question, because you knew she had a good reason and you trusted her. You couldn't help but respect someone who could do what she could do with a dog. If she told a dog to stand on its hind legs, it did. You had to respect someone who had that much love and control of what she was doing. She never doubted herself, never doubted the dog. If she handled the dog, it was a good dog. That left no doubt in other peoples' eyes that she had the best dog."

Ms. Willis continues, "I don't care whether it was a Chihuahua or Great Dane, she showed it on a loose lead; the dog just adored her. She had its undivided attention. I truly believe she could train a mouse to stack. There's just something about her. She has a certain presence. She is the very best."

Ms. Willis tells a story about how her Malamute took care of Adelene. "When she fell once in the ring, my Malamute would not let anyone get near her. She couldn't get up. My dog loved people, but he would not let anyone come near her until she told him it was OK. Finally, someone was able to help her up and take the dog. He adored her. Dogs knew that she loved them, and they performed for her."

Another of Adelene's former clients, John Ed Lee, for whom she showed the nation's top-winning Dalmatian bitch in 1973, states, "Her knowledge of breed standards and overall ring presentation is a benchmark in dog circles throughout the south."

Top professional handler Carl Sanders has known Adelene since 1973. He confides, "One of the most memorable things she did for me was teach me how to stack the first dog I showed. People kept saying that the dog looked wrong, so she showed me how to stack him so that he looked right. That was her secret and my secret. He was an Afghan, and he held the record for winning specialties for several years." He continues, "She was one of the top-notch handlers in this area and is known all over the country.

She was hard to beat in Texas, no matter what she was handling. She worked hard at handling. She is a true professional." He adds, "You were always aware of her presence. She made you look at her. She just had an aura about her."

Retired professional all-breed handler Roy Murray comments, "Adelene and I had a lot of fun showing dogs. We got to be better friends because in the ring, we would do what I called 'running a trailer.' Adelene had a dog that would act up in the ring if someone got too close behind her, so I would get in the Group ring first and save her a place in front of me. Then I would be sure not to crowd her. Adelene always had a place at the front of the line. We used to make some people unhappy because I was letting her in front of me, but that way no one could bother her dog. We became great friends because of that and have been for years."

Mr. Murray notes that Adelene was always very competitive in the ring. "When you went in the ring with her, she was the one you had to beat." He recalls, "I was showing a Weimaraner that was competition for Adelene. I told the owner not to come near the ring because if the dog saw her, he would go crazy. Well, the dog saw the owner and was going crazy, so I just turned him loose. He ran out of the ring and over to the owner. The judge told me to go get the dog. I brought the dog back into the ring, showed it and beat Adelene that day. Adelene was so angry that after she left the ring, she won the American Staffordshire National Specialty in another ring. She said she was so mad nobody was going to beat her."

Adelene enjoys telling the following story. "One time I was in the Basset ring, and there were two female handlers behind me and a male handler ahead of me. The girl just behind me would roll her dog's front (moving the dog's head, neck and chest as a unit from side to side) to show that the elbows were real tight against the body. So I'd roll my dog's front too. We kept doing it;

finally the judge announced that he could see what we were showing. When we came out of the ring, the male handler told me he didn't dare turn around because he didn't know what I was showing off."

Adelene enjoyed competing in the Malamute ring against her good friends John and LouAnn Penland of Pine Bluff, Arkansas. She states, "I knew John's dog would jump around if it heard another dog growl, so I taught my dog to growl so softly that no one could hear him except John's dog. Then John's dog would act up, and of course, we'd win." When they would come out of the ring, Mr. Penland would always hug Adelene and say, "I know you're doing something, you old heifer, but I don't know what." They became fast friends, and Adelene taught John how to handle his dog. "Then it took something to beat him because he did have a lovely dog. He went on to win many Breeds and Group placements," she says.

Great Handlers and Judges

Years ago, at the Houston Kennel Club show in the Coliseum, we were in the Sporting Group. I was first in line with my Weimar, Roy Murray was right behind me with an Irish Setter and Dorothy Nickles was judging. Ms. Nickles went over my Weimar, and when she took hold of the Irish Setter's muzzle, I leaned over my dog's rear like I was setting it up again and said, "Hail Mary, full of grace, put Roy in second place." Dorothy stepped back and cut those eyes at me as only Dorothy can do, and of course, Roy was laughing and practically falling over his dog. She went on with the judging, and I won that night. Afterward Dorothy commented that she "wasn't going to go against Heaven." She tells this story when she's making speeches at banquets and other events, and she keeps adding to it. She even says that I dropped to my knees and a light came from Heaven. So it's been a lot of fun. Dorothy's acquaintances all know how she makes life so much fun.

Adelene first met Dorothy Nickles when showing under her in obedience. She states, "Dorothy Nickles is a very strong, dignified, great lady." Adelene notes that Ms. Nickles is a good person for a novice to get to know. "All you have to do is introduce yourself as a novice; I guarantee she'll aim you in the right direction. She has done that for thousands of people in this business. She was always kind to me, but she also put me through some real trials."

One of those trials occurred when Adelene and Duchess were showing to Ms. Nickles in open obedience. Adelene recalls, "It was the exercise where the dog retrieved the dumbell over the high jump. I threw the dumbell, but Dorothy didn't think it went far enough, so she had me throw it again. Dorothy still didn't think I had thrown it far enough. I threw it again, and it almost flew out of the ring. She told me to send Duchess, and of course, Duchess did a good job and brought it back to me. The people outside the ring said Dorothy was just trying to mess me up, but in my opinion, she just made Duchess look good because Duchess sat and waited for the command to go over the jump. She didn't break on her sit-stay until I gave her the command, and that made Duchess look good."

When Adelene and Duchess attended an obedience seminar Dorothy conducted in San Antonio, Dorothy put Adelene to another test. "She had me with Duchess and Barbara Brown, a lovely girl and a good dog trainer with a Doberman Pinscher, do the seek-back. In those days you carried a leather glove, and the judge would tell you to drop it. She'd have the dogs heel and sit in a pattern; then she would tell you to do an about-turn and send the dog out to get the glove. The dog always knew it was out there because that's the way they were trained. She had our dogs heel and sit; then we returned to a certain point where the dogs' backs were to the gloves."

Because her back was turned, Adelene was unaware that Dorothy had taken Duchess' glove, walked quite a distance to the wall and stuck the glove under some wood lying against the wall. Then Dorothy asked them to do an about-turn and said, "Send the Weimaraner." Adelene gave Duchess the command to get the glove. "And of course, my eyes were frantically looking at the ground, trying to find it. I knew where I dropped it, but it wasn't there." Adelene remembers thinking, "If she embarrasses my Duchess, I'll kill her!" But Duchess went out a few feet, smelled and stepped back a couple of steps. She smelled again, turned and trotted over to the wall, pulled the wood back, got the glove and came trotting back. Adelene continued, "Duchess sat in front of me and delivered it to my hand. Dorothy told me to finish, and when I told Duchess to heel, she went around to the heel position." Then Dorothy said, "Ladies and gentlemen, you have just seen a dog use her nose."

Gabby and Tony Gwinner, outstanding Weimaraner breeders and handlers from California, had a profound impact on Lou and Adelene Pardo. Through traveling and working with the Gwinners, the Pardos absorbed a vast amount of knowledge, wisdom and experience.

Adelene recalls, "Gabby Gwinner was a wonderful lady with the cutest laugh. Once at judges' dinner in Longview, she was telling us that when she and Tony were first married, he said he didn't want his wife to work. Gabby was laughing because she ran a big boarding kennel at Mission Valley in San Diego, California, and she traveled with Tony to the shows and did all the grooming. She was working 10 times harder running a kennel and being a handler's assistant than she ever did being a housewife."

Adelene fondly recalls another story about Tony. "Tony Gwinner, God love him, was not a mechanic. And he didn't know a thing about motor homes. One time while they were staying with us between shows, his motor home needed front-end alignment work. We could not find a mechanic because it was a front-wheel-drive motor home, so a lot of garages couldn't do it. Tony made things worse by telling the mechanics how to do the work, so other places would also refuse to do it. Finally, I realized that I should take him to my own mechanic, but I told him that if he uttered one word I was going to shoot him."

She continues, "My mechanic repaired his motor home, but I was mad at Tony for wasting so much time trying to boss the mechanics around. Finally, we were on our way. Gabby was in the back, knitting, which is what she did when Tony and I were fighting about something. She knitted a lot because we were always fussing in a family sort of way. Tony asked how to find a certain restaurant that served popcorn shrimp because he knew I loved them. He figured if he took me to lunch, I wouldn't be mad at him anymore. I told him he wasn't going to get on my good side by feeding me popcorn shrimp, but he took us to lunch anyway.

"Tony Gwinner was a lovely man, and they were a lovely couple. They're gone now, but not a day goes by that I don't miss them," she states.

Adelene remembers another incident that occurred on the Texas Circuit. The Gwinners, the Pardos and two or three other handlers were driving in a caravan from Harlingen to Corpus Christi when Tony stopped at a restaurant. They all went in and ordered food that was simple and quick to cook. She says, "We sat there and sat there, waiting for our orders. I know we sat there an hour. We were all dead tired, sitting and leaning on the table and talking." Adelene decided to peek through the little glass window to the kitchen and discovered that the cook had suddenly quit and the owner was frantically trying to get their orders cooked. "We all laughed later about how we were so tired that we just sat there and waited all that time instead of going to another restaurant."

Throughout their show careers the Pardos encountered many of the country's top handlers. They competed with and became friends with Harry Sangster and his helper, Corky Vroom; Larry Downey and his helper, Clay Cody; the Rodwells; Norton and Betty Moore; Ric Chashoudian; Chuck Hamilton; Dorothy Nickles; Derek Rayne; and many other prominent handlers, breeders and judges. Adelene adds, "In those days everyone would sit around the Group ring and talk about the dogs as they came in. And Chuck Hamilton would talk about his training of the K-9 dogs during World War II.

"Harry Sangster could make a dog come up on its pasterns prettier than anyone I've ever seen," Adelene comments. She would joke that he must have burned the bottoms of their pasterns so they would stand up on their toes.

And she marveled at Stan Flowers' magnificent hands. "When you watch his hands, the way he touches a dog, the way he sets them up, you know that he's extremely good at it and knows the business."

Adelene knew that Roy Murray kept a mysterious substance in a yellow mustard bottle. When he groomed Wirehaired Dachshunds or German Wirehaired Pointers, he would rub some in his hands and then put it on the coat. "He said it was some kind of magic," she says. "For years I'd ask him what it was, and he would always say it was magic. I told him it smelled like Jergens lotion, but he'd deny it, telling me it was his magic mix. He didn't tell me until he retired, a few years ago, what it was—Jergens lotion. He used it to make the coat feel wiry.

"Larry Downey taught me to apply chalk properly using his Boxer, Standing Ovation, a great dog in those days." Chalk is applied as part of the grooming routine for certain breeds. She continues, "Larry came on the Texas circuit one year and won Best in Show on Saturday with a Boxer and Best in Show the next day with the dog's brother. After that I always wanted to have brothers that won Best in Show. I knew I couldn't do it on two days like he did, but it was always my dream to have brothers that won Best in Show. Dago and Starwar were brothers and they were Best in Show winners. So I did get my dream. If you work for your dreams, you'll make it."

Dog Show Stories

On a trip to Mississippi, the motor home engine would miss when the headlights were turned on. The engine would run fine if we used just the running lights. I really wanted to get to Mississippi because the two scheduled judges loved the dog that I was showing; I said, "If I have to carry this motor home, I'm getting there." So I lay on the dashboard and shined two flashlights on the center white line of the highway while Lou drove. We stopped about half way at a service station, which was closed, since it was midnight or so. I called the police to ask for help; they came and helped us fix the motor home.

The dog show world is a subculture rich in stories and adventures. This abundance of tales and legends results from the wide variety of people who attend and compete, the diversity and number of dogs attending the shows and the necessary travel and other logistics involved in showing. Through her 42 years of participation in dog shows and quite possibly because of her intense personality, Mrs. Pardo has accumulated a wealth of anecdotes. She states, "To this day, people still ask if I remember a match from years ago. Of course, this is the old timers talking, but I do remember and hold these experiences deep in my heart."

Adelene tells a story about Duchess when she won a fun match sponsored by the Houston Kennel Club at the Sears parking lot on South Main around 1961. Duchess won Best of Breed and the Sporting Group. "It got real late—maybe 2:00 A.M.—and the lights at Sears went out, but they still had to judge Best in Match. Everyone made a big circle with their cars and turned the headlights on. That's how we finished the match."

She recalls a Houston Kennel Club show in October 1969 in the Pin Oak Horse Show Arena near the 610 Loop and Highway 59. "The show rings were in the horse show arena, which had tanbark on the ground. It rained cats and dogs the night before; then it started flooding. Everyone put on his raincoat, hat and boots. The tanbark had stopped up the drains, and the arena started filling up like a bowl. The arena was full of water; it came up to about my lower calves. I was showing a Basset for a client, and you could not see the dog's undercarriage because the water was so deep. The client was showing a Basset puppy that had to swim into the ring because he wasn't as tall as the older dogs."

She continues, "They had fewer absentees in that show than they ever had previously. They showed the toy breeds up in the stands to keep them out of the weather. When I showed my Weimaraner Thunderwheel, he kept his eyes closed when he was in a show stance because the rain was beating on his face so hard he couldn't keep them open. The Afghans were so wet that you could actually see their structure. When it was all over that day and I took off all my rain gear, the only thing that was wet was a little piece of my hair. We had a good time. People who were there still laugh about how deep the water was in that horse arena.

"I was showing the number one Dalmatian bitch in the nation one year at an outdoor show in Enid, Oklahoma. The bitch's father was number one in that breed. We went in the specials ring, and there were maybe five specials. The judge said, 'Take them around,' and we took them around. He pointed at my dog and said 'You're Best of Breed,' and I got my ribbon and went back to the motor home. He did not move or go over any of the specials. He just had us go around the ring. That was the easiest Best of Breed I ever won."

Adelene laughs at herself when recalling, "I handled a Basenji bitch for Tom and Nancy Pincus that had to have some medicine every day. I took the capsule apart and gave her the powder. She sat there, looked at me and spit it out. When she did, I happened to have my mouth open—like I always do—and the powder went right down my throat. So I actually took the powder for her that day."

Every year since Tony Gwinner passed away, a perpetual memorial trophy is given in his name at the Reliant Park (formerly Astrohall) shows. Adelene is honored to present it at the Sporting Group competition. She created quite a stir at ringside one year, as she recalls, "You have to dress formally for the Groups. I'd always ask Roy Murray if I could hang my clothes in his motor home so they'd stay cool during the day. If I left them in my car, they would get so hot in July and August I wouldn't be able to put them on. Roy always kept an Irish Setter, a real guard dog, loose in the motor home. You didn't dare go in if she was there. She didn't bite when you came in, but she bit you as you went out. One year I went to the ring where Roy was showing and asked for the keys to the motor home. I asked, 'Is the alligator in there?' He told me no, but several people around the ring overheard and thought that Roy really kept an alligator in his motor home.

"Years ago at the shows, they would call the dogs to the ring by CB radio. If they needed Poodle dog number six to ring five, for example, they would announce the number and the ring. At a show in Corpus Christi, they called some bitches to the ring. Suddenly, a voice sounded from one of the ringside radios, giving his location on a boat in the ocean near Corpus Christi. The voice announced, 'If you-all have got any of those bitches left, you can send them out here.' "

Adelene recalls some humorous incidents involving handlers. "Years ago we were in Las Cruces, New Mexico, working for Tony. One of the handlers had a little baby goat she kept in an exercise pen. It looked like a little toy. Some of the other handlers decided she should bring it in the ring, so she took it to the end of the line. Hollis Wilson came in to judge the Terriers, went over that goat and let her move it. Mr. Wilson was just as calm as a kitten and never blinked an eye, acting just like that goat was a dog. He judged the whole class, everybody went out and we all laughed. If you did that today, you'd be in big trouble but we used to have some really fun times."

She recalls another incident when several handlers used wire to reinforce the leads and collars and showed invisible dogs. "The wire made it look like the dogs were really there, and the judge went all through the judging as if he could see the dogs. Of course, that was back in the days when you had three rings at a dog show and one of them was obedience. The total entry would be about 300 dogs, so there was more time for fun."

There is a dog show somewhere in the United States nearly every weekend of the year. Many shows are scheduled in "clusters," with more than one area kennel club sponsoring two to five shows in the same location over a weekend. Many of the professional handlers, breeders and exhibitors travel with their dogs to the shows in motor homes and camp out on or near the show grounds. Retired handler Roy Murray calls this phenomenon "tracing the white stripe." Most fanciers traveling in motor homes tell amusing anecdotes about the breakdown of their motor homes; Adelene is no exception. From 1971 to 1981, as she and Lou traveled by motor home to the shows, Lou became known as an expert motor home mechanic.

"The great Poodle handler Bobby Peeples used to always say that when you bought a motor home, it should come furnished with a 'Lou,' so that when the motor home broke down, he would be there to fix it." Adelene liked to say, "There's nothing deader than a broken motor home sitting on the side of the road."

Adelene continues, "Our motor home, I can truthfully say, never did leave us stranded. I always said that my motor home ran on my mother's prayers because she always prayed for us from the time we left to the time we returned. We had things break on the motor home, but we'd always be on the lot at the dog show or just driving in the driveway when it fell apart." She recalls one instance when their priest blessed the motor home and Thunderwheel, who was resting in his customary position on the motor cover.

She remembers, "We were heading out of Houston on I-45 on the way to Tulsa. Lou always drove until we got out of Houston; when I took over, the steering wheel started shaking. Lou got the flashlight and looked at the tires. All except one or two lug nuts had come off the left rear duals, and the wheels were about to come off. We chugged along about half a mile to a service station and asked for the mechanic. But Billy Bob had gone to a ball game."

She continues, "We had a dog named Johnny Walker that was real cute and loved to play with kids. I figured we needed to get Billy Bob home from the ballgame, so I got Johnny Walker out and let him play with the kids. Finally, the man said he'd go see if he could find Billy Bob. Meanwhile, another worker took Lou to town to find the lug bolts, came back and pulled the axle. The two men did all that, and Billy Bob came home from the ballgame just because Johnny Walker made those kids happy.

"With the wheels repaired, we finally set off for Tulsa," she concluded. "I was afraid the repair bill would be $300 and I was going to make the client pay. But they only charged us $27.50. The reason we just had to get to Tulsa was that my client's dog needed one point to finish. He had entered it in Open on Saturday and as a champion on Sunday. So I had to get there on Saturday to try to win that point. Well, we did get there; I did win the point."

Adelene chuckles about how Roy Murray gave her a lesson in weather forecasting. Rainy weather during a show presents special challenges for those who need to care for and exercise the dogs. She notes, "I always got up very early in the morning to get all my work done and get dressed. So I'd be out in the rain under the awnings, getting the dogs in and out of the motor home and trying to keep them dry. I noticed that Roy would never come out until the sun came up and it never would be raining." One day Roy explained, "Adelene, you just need to wait until the break of dawn. Even when its raining real hard, it always stops at the first light." Adelene started observing this weather phenomenon and took Roy's advice. "From then on, I waited until the first light before I started exercising my dogs. It made things a lot easier."

Adelene recalls another motor home story involving a handler friend who had borrowed someone's motor home to drive to Little Rock, Arkansas. "The motor home's awning kept coming unsnapped and would completely unfurl while they were driving. They'd have to stop, roll it back up, clip all the clips, tie all the ties, then start off again. Another mile or so and down it would come. So they drove from just outside of Houston all the way to Little Rock with that awning unfurling every so often."

She notes, "Back in those days, you'd go to a dog show and show your dogs, then you'd pack up all your exercise pens and gear and you might have to drive 250 miles to the next show, which was the next day. People blessed with four or five shows in one place don't understand the amount of work we used to do, going from one show location to the other.

"Sometimes you would just get nutty because you were so tired, hauling it down the road from one dog show to the other," she states. Once, as she and Lou drove their motor home from a show in Amarillo to some big shows in California, Adelene came down with a severe migraine headache. She told Lou she felt really sick and asked him to pull off the road, but the road had no shoulders and there was no place to stop. The pain finally became too much for Adelene and in her delirium, she attempted to go out the door while the motor home was still moving. On the way out the door, her arm caught on the dinette furniture, saving her life. Lou took her straight to a hospital; three days later she was back handling dogs.

She relates another incident involving impaired judgment. "Two handlers were driving their motor homes to a show, talking to each other on the CB radio. One handler apparently needed to get something from the other handler, but instead of stopping to exchange the item, the handler's helper opened the motor home door and was trying to pass it between motor homes as they were speeding down the road. The helper slipped and fell out onto the highway with those two motor homes flying down the road side by side."

The Texas show circuit in the 1960s and 1970s usually involved eight shows in a 10-day period, with shows in Austin, San Antonio, Harlingen, McAllen, Corpus Christi, Galveston, Houston, Shreveport, Longview, Dallas and Fort Worth. The Pardos spent several years on the Texas circuit assisting the Gwinners. One year in McAllen, Tony Gwinner took Adelene along for one of his favorite activities: grocery shopping. "He was worse than a woman about shopping," she laughs. They took grocery orders from the other handlers and set off for the store, which was located across a 4- or 5-acre field from the show grounds. Someone gave them a lift to the store, and after they had filled the grocery orders, Tony decided they should haul all the groceries back in a grocery cart across the shortest route, directly across the furrowed field.

"Being a good handler's helper, I did as I was told, and across the plowed field we went, with me pulling on the cart and Tony pushing." Adelene notes, "All the way across I was telling Tony that we couldn't take the basket, since it was against the law, and Tony was laughing the whole time." She chuckles, "When Tony got it in his mind he wanted to do something, well, we did it. And people loved him so much they'd do anything he wanted. So I just went very obediently along, and we got across that field, laughing and hollering and carrying on, with me telling Tony we shouldn't be doing it." They crossed the field, delivered all the groceries and put the cart in the trunk of someone's car to take it back to the store.

She smiles as she recalls her experiences working with the Gwinners. "When we were helping Tony, we'd set up the exercise pens and put up the little water buckets. Tony always wanted the buckets half full." One day he came to the setup to find everything spic and span and everyone busy working. "Tony said he wanted the buckets half empty, and I told him they were half full. And he said, 'I didn't say I wanted them half full, I said I wanted them half empty.' And then he just died laughing." Adelene laughs, "That's one of the silly little things he would do to us all the time. We would always send him somewhere to get him out of our hair so we could go on with the grooming and the rest of our work."

She relates another story. "Mama Kit (Ch. Cati v. d. Gretchen-hof), Gabby's bitch out of the Gretchenhof line, produced some really good litters. One year in McAllen, we were busy in the rings; Gabby left Mama Kit in the motor home and shut the screen door. While we were working, Mama Kit pushed open the door and walked all the way to downtown McAllen. Someone identified her as a show dog and brought her back to the show building. There was an announcement that there was a Weimar bitch waiting for her owner at the superintendent's desk. Gabby and I knew it was Mama Kit. I don't know if Gabby ever told Tony that Mama Kit had wandered away; he would have killed both of us if anything had happened to her. She was a sweetheart, but she was a typical Weimar in that she always let you know that she had the last word."

Another Texas circuit story involves Roy Murray. "We were in the Sporting Group at the Galveston Kennel Club one March; Roy was showing a German Wirehaired Pointer named Rudy that was a super dog." As the handlers and dogs were moving around the ring, Roy slipped and fell on the slick floor. She continues, "Of course, he let go of the lead and the other handlers kept going. Rudy just went right on around the ring as if Roy was right there with him. Roy got up and waited, and when Rudy passed him, he just picked up the lead and away they went. The dog showed himself all the way around the ring. Just shows you what the words 'show dog' mean."

One year on the Texas circuit at a show in Harlingen, when the temperature was in the 30s, a handler was going out to walk a Borzoi. "Just as he got out the door, the blast of cold air spooked the Borzoi and she took off running," Adelene relates. Borzois are noted for their quickness and running speed; this bitch was so fast that no one around the show grounds could catch her. "The handler was about to die," Adelene recalls. Just then, Lou arranged to borrow a car from one of Adelene's clients so he could get cigarettes. Adelene knew that Lou wasn't worried about getting cigarettes; he was worried about that Borzoi and the handler. She adds, "We all know how it feels when one of your charges gets away. It makes you sick inside." Lou rode around in the car until he spotted the Borzoi. He stopped the car, opened the door and called out to her, but the Borzoi took off running again. Lou followed her to a railroad crossing where a train was moving on the tracks. He watched the Borzoi rocking back and forth, as if she was getting into the rhythm of the wheels and figuring how much room she would have to get under that train. "Sure enough, she ran right under the moving train to the other side."

After the train passed, Lou started following the Borzoi again and watched her run through the gates of a factory. Lou followed her inside, jumped out and closed the gates. Then he went to the office and ascertained that the factory was completely enclosed by the fence. He explained to the employees what had happened and asked permission to look for the dog. "Lou went all over, looking around everything in that big plant, but he couldn't find her. Finally he noticed the door ajar on one of the portable toilets and found the Borzoi sitting on the toilet. Of course, she was growling at him. But her lead was hanging down in front, so he just reached his hand in as quietly as he could. When he took hold of the lead, she came right out with no problems whatsoever." Lou brought the Borzoi back to the grateful handler. "He's retired from handling, but to this day, whenever Lou needs something, he can get it from this man because he saved the Borzoi."

She relates another remarkable incident that happened later that same day. A white Bull Terrier got away from his handler, ran out in the street and was hit by a car. Adelene relates, "But the Bull Terrier, being so stocky, well-built and in good condition, wasn't injured, so he just got right back up." The driver stopped his car, and several people in the area were trying unsuccessfully to catch the dog. "Lou opened the back door of the car, hoping the dog would jump in. Well, he did, and the driver jumped right out when that big Bull Terrier jumped in. In South Texas at that time, I don't think many people had seen a dog of that breed. He was white as snow, but now he had black tire marks on him." The handler rushed the dog back into the show building; almost immediately, they called the Terrier Group to the ring. Adelene laughs, "The handler didn't have time to clean the tire marks off, but they won the Terrier Group that night anyway. And Lou made another dear friend because he helped catch the dog."

Adelene and Lou laugh about many of their traveling adventures. During one trip, Adelene and Benny Conboy persuaded Lou to pull off the road in a snow storm, but only after he had driven up and down the highway a couple of miles in each direction in an attempt to locate the best television reception so they could watch a movie in the motor home. Ordering pie at a truck stop and mistakenly grabbing a bag with someone else's hamburger, blowing out the motor home's television by plugging it into the wrong voltage at the direction of a friend, and many similar incidents provided amusement and comic relief to the weary dog show travelers.

Adelene recalls some fun times she had with her first client as a licensed professional handler. "Bob Arbs was my first paying client, and because he sold heavy equipment, he was able to follow me around to the shows. Wherever I went to show his dogs, he would arrive, sell a few machines and then come to the show." At the time Adelene was traveling alone because Lou couldn't get off work, so Bob would help her pick up droppings and put out the exercise pens. "I would joke that I had the richest kennel boy of all the handlers. He wore $300 and $400 suits and there he was, picking up droppings in those suits."

One year Adelene attended a show in Wichita Falls, Texas, in a building called the Purple Onion. She says, "I think it was a dance hall; we were all driving around, trying to find it. Bob Arbs was driving in front of me and Gene Blake and Bobby Peeples were behind. When you see someone that you know on the road and you're having a hard time finding the building, you follow each other. We had a regular caravan going and we couldn't find the Purple Onion. Finally, Bob stopped in the middle of the street and said that he didn't know where the building was, but the address was at that spot. So we started looking around; out across the pasture was a little dinky building. Sure enough, that was the Purple Onion." After the caravan stopped, Bob accused Adelene of driving 80 miles an hour. Adelene argued that she never drove over the 70-mph speed limit. Bob told her that every car he rented must have a broken speedometer, because it always appeared that Adelene was driving 80. Later Adelene discovered that Lou had put larger tires on her van that caused the speedometer to indicate the wrong speed.

Adelene remembers having a big disagreement with Mr. Arbs about breeding dogs. She explains, "Bob was a highly educated man. He was always reading books and studying. He came over to the kennel and said he couldn't get these two Bassets bred. We got the dog and bitch out, but the bitch didn't want to have anything to do with the dog and the dog wasn't paying much attention to her. So I told Bob they were just not ready and that he should wait until tomorrow morning and try again. If it didn't work in the morning, then he should try again in the afternoon." Bob said that his vet had checked the bitch and said that it was time to breed. His books all said the same thing. Adelene replied that he should pay attention to the dogs. "Sometimes you have to lay the book down and use common sense. If the two dogs are not paying any attention to each other, they are not going to breed," she said. Adelene predicted that it would be two more days before they would breed.

Adelene and Bob continued to argue. "He went home in a huff. He and I were always having some kind of heated argument. We were like family. He went home saying that his book said to breed on that day and they were going to breed. He called me that night and we argued again. I told him that I was right and slammed the phone down." The entire telephone conversation had been accidentally recorded on Adelene's answering machine. A couple days later he called Adelene to tell her the Bassets had bred. "Actually, they bred on the very day I said they would," she laughs. "I kept the recording on that machine. Every time we got into it about who was right and who was wrong, I would play that recording to him so he would remember who knew how to breed dogs. Bob is gone now, but he was a lovely man, had a lovely wife and children and we sure do miss him."

On Teaching

*O*nce when I was judging, I asked an exhibitor to
move her dog in a triangle. The woman replied,
"I can't do that. I haven't had that lesson in class yet."

Adelene started teaching soon after she started showing dogs. She first conducted classes in conformation and obedience among some friends in what is now a parking lot at Meyerland Plaza in Houston. Finally, one of her students suggested she should charge for her knowledge. She notes, "I look around at shows now and think that I have probably trained 85% of the people in the building, or I have trained their mothers or their grandmothers."

When she teaches someone in conformation or obedience, she begins by watching the dog, not the person. She notes, "The dog tells me what the handler is doing." She continues, "When I'm training someone, I look into their eyes. I ask people not to wear sunglasses, because I look into their eyes to tell whether they understand."

Mrs. Pardo's students arrive for their lessons anticipating the closest of scrutiny. They know that nothing will escape her sharp eyes and they must do their best. An air of seriousness and concentration pervades her classes, but she also is careful to allow time to relax and share some humor. The students enjoy hearing stories of her adventures in showing dogs.

She is constantly pointing out how a dog thinks and showing how to interpret the dog's actions. In the words of Anne Page, one of Adelene's former students, ". . . she teaches her students how to 'think' like their dogs, how to interpret their actions, and how to use that knowledge to help the shy, unruly or inexperienced dog adapt to the show ring."

As a result of attending outdoor classes year-round, her students are able to show their dogs in rain or sun, oppressive heat or extreme cold. Studying with Adelene includes wiping large drops of perspiration off the dog's back in July and learning to handle while wearing earmuffs and gloves. It is all part of Adelene's philosophy of preparing for any possibility.

At the start of every class, she asks for "brags" from the students. Many of them report they have won points or finished their dogs at shows the previous weekend. But even the smaller victories, like winning a class, are praised before the students begin working.

Some of Adelene's notable students include David Harper, the 1985 Westminster Best Junior Handler; Sandra League, who handled one of the all-time winning American Staffordshire Terriers; and Jill and Russell Drennan.

Carolyn Willis noted, "I trusted her with my most prized possession, my child, Sandra League. She trained my child. I turned her over to Adelene at eight years of age. Adelene never let me down, ever. My daughter is a professional handler today because of Adelene Pardo."

After studying with Mrs. Pardo, Ms. League showed her all-time winning American Staffordshire Terrier, Ch. Sultan's Wild Card ("Bubba"), to his first National Specialty championship in 1996 at 18 months of age. Two years later Bubba and Sandra won the largest National Specialty in the history of the breed. Sandra adds, "If she hadn't taught me, I would never have survived in dogs. But she made it fun. She taught me to take my dog and show it to the judge like it is the best apple in the world and I am selling it. She taught me to think I'm the best handler and I've got the best dog."

Adelene's students, many of whom are professional handlers, place a high premium on her honesty. As one states, "I knew I had to work hard and do well so she wouldn't throw me out of class. She doesn't waste time with students who do not work hard or have no talent. That was a confidence builder because as long as she let me continue in her class, I knew I was doing well. If she told me I was doing a good job, I knew it was the truth and that she wasn't just being polite. It was an honor when she asked me to demonstrate something to the rest of the class."

Ms. Willis confirms, "She's so honest. She's honest about everything she does." Other students remark on her ability to cut through to the root of a problem. "She once told me that if I didn't stop my nervous laugh I'd never finish a dog," one noted. Adelene would call that common sense, but a psychiatrist would probably have a more detailed and costly analysis.

Mrs. Pardo firmly believes that dogs are like children and should be taught good manners. She says, "If you want him to have good manners, you have to teach him. He'll respect you all the more for taking the time to teach him." Her constant key word is "respect," and her philosophy of training dogs equates respect with love. "Teach the dog to respect you," she says. "When he loves and respects you, he'll climb mountains, walk through fire, even give his life for you." Just as her students know they are expected to work hard, they know their dogs are expected to show good manners in class and at shows.

One of her seminar students wrote the following letter:

Dear Mrs. Pardo:

I entered the best Boston Terrier I have ever bred.

I wore a blouse, skirt and suit jacket.

I wore shoes that tied so they would not fall off.

I had a big piece of bait that the dog could see.

I hung back until I could show my dog's gait properly in spite of the slow movers in front of us.

I created a frame around myself and my dog.

I thanked the judge for her instructions.

I did everything Adelene Pardo taught me to do in her two-day seminar in Phoenix.

At the Boston Terrier Club of America's National Specialty Show on April 1st and 2nd at the Safari Hotel in Scottsdale, Arizona under breeder/judge Maryann Caruso, with an entry of 180 dogs, Nans Cors Fletch of Willow Hill went Winners Dog and Best of Winners. You may remember he snored a little in your class but he picked up quite a few tips.

Thank you Mrs. Pardo.

Most gratefully,

Corinne Connell

On Judging

W hen you go in the ring to judge, you have no friends. When I first started judging, people who called me "friend" didn't talk to me after I judged. One girl was very angry because I did not put her dogs up just because I knew her. I told her, "When you ate at my table you had bad dogs, when I taught you to handle you had bad dogs and you've still got bad dogs."

For Adelene, becoming a judge was a natural progression from being a good handler and breeder. "When I started into dogs, I knew I wanted to go all the way. I watched great handlers from the past become judges; I wanted to do the same thing," she states. "Whether it was selling defense stamps or picking up scrap iron as we did during World War II, or campaigning in junior high to get my candidate elected queen of the annual May fête, I always wanted to go forward and learn things and do my best."

She notes that going from handling to judging requires an attitude adjustment. "When you handle a dog, you are trying to be the winner. You are trying to sell the apple to the judge. You're trying to convince them that your dog is the best apple," she states, adding, "When you're handling, you've got the attitude that you're going to win. You've been working hard with your dog, and you've done everything that has to be done. I call that doing your job."

Adelene recalls asking some of the more experienced judges, "When you judge, you're not trying to beat anybody, so what gold am I looking for? And one of the old judges—the masters, I call them—told me that I should be looking for that one great dog. He said that a good judge wants to be the first to find the great Sporting dog, or the great Working dog." The first judge to find a great dog and put him up for Winners is able to claim, "Well, I gave that Cocker his first win and now he's number one in the nation, so I must have known what I was doing." Adelene likes to say, "AKC ought to be happy with me. That dog I picked is number one in the nation."

She continues, "I wanted to breed good dogs, show good dogs and have winning dogs. I never minded working because hard work is what makes you rise to the top. I always went to the old folks and asked them questions to learn, because I figured they had walked the walk. They were going to lead me around some hard times because they had already passed through. I became a handler because of the encouragement of Tony and Gabby Gwinner. Tony always said I had a natural ability to handle dogs and that I should be a handler. And of course, after handling is judging."

Adelene admired many of the great judges, including Dorothy Nickles, Chuck Hamilton, Derek Rayne, Gordon Parham, Percy Roberts, Al Vary, and Esme and Al Treen. She learned from talking with these great judges, noting, "They were all lovely people. They would always take time to sit and talk with you about judging, about dogs, and I learned a lot from them. Tony always said that you should try to help people, and when you go into judging, you should try very hard to be a good judge and to do what's right."

Years ago, many people told Adelene she had a natural eye for good dogs. "They say you either have it or you don't. But I think you can develop a good eye by reading the standards, watching the judges, talking to people, sitting at the Group ring, and listening to judges talk with each other about dogs." Analyzing and understanding which dogs the judges "put up," or award the points and Best of Winners, will help the student learn proportions, structure and type.

She adds, "Of course, when I first started in dogs, the show was only three rings and one of them was obedience, so the judges had a lot more time to sit and talk. Now it isn't really possible, but I used to sit with the judges and talk and listen. I loved to sit with Derek and Chuck and all the other greats when the Groups were on and talk about the different breeds. To this day I have never forgotten the things they taught me. That's truly the way you learn."

She continues, "You can read it in books, you can go to seminars, you can go to all kinds of study groups. But it's better to sit beside someone who is very knowledgeable, listen to him, ask questions and try to learn. The key word is 'listen.' Don't tell them about it. Listen to them and remember."

According to Adelene, the first thing the judge should look for in judging a dog is breed type. Type refers to the fine points of the breed standard as they apply to the general appearance of each dog. Type normally is defined in the first paragraph of each breed standard as set out in the AKC's *The Complete Dog Book*.

She notes, "You want to pick type first, and then you've got to have the soundness. They go together like jelly and bread, like peanut butter and crackers. I was always taught that when a dog moves well, all his structural parts are in the right place."

"You can't miss it," she notes. "I don't care if it's a Chihuahua, a Weimaraner or a Great Dane. If they're sound, they're sound. Soundness means that they move with no lost motion. It means that they're clean coming and going, that their elbows are not flying. If you want to know if a dog has a bad front, don't look at it coming toward you. Look at it going away from you. When you see elbows flying out on either side of the body, you know that the shoulders are not what they're supposed to be. If you see a dog with a real short neck, you know that the shoulders are not where they're supposed to be. But when you look at a dog, look at the whole dog; don't just look at one part of it."

She adds, "When you're judging a dog on movement, the dog should be moving from one point to the other as effortlessly as possible. A lot of people today think that movement is speed, but it is not speed. It's no lost action, no lost motion. Just a well-balanced dog, covering ground."

Adelene stresses that a good judge knows the breed standard, balance, height, movement and type. She adds, "It's hard to teach someone all the things that they need to know about dogs. Many people believe that a good eye for dogs has to be born in you. But you just have to learn to look at the overall dog to see the balance, to see the whole animal.

"You're judging breeding stock, so you want to find the best of that breed and compare it to the standard of that particular breed. Some people, when they talk dogs or judge, only talk about one thing; maybe they'll judge the head or the rear. But when you judge a dog, you should look at the whole dog." She cites as an example a puppy belonging to one of her students. "Unless I miss my guess, he's going to be one heck of a dog. The overall balance of the dog, the way the neck goes into the shoulders, the way the tail sits on the body, is a sight to behold."

A good judge appreciates type as it relates to function or how the dog works and how he does the job that he was bred to do. Adelene notes, "For instance, take a Sporting dog. When people go hunting, they may hunt for eight hours at a time, and that dog is out in front of them going back and forth, traveling a lot more ground than the hunter. So a good Sporting dog has to be structurally sound to hold up to that. The judge must ask whether a dog can go all day long hunting birds, or whether he will give out because the structure is not proper." She cites another example in the Afghan hound. "The Afghan hound was born to run over rock and rough terrain, so the judge needs to ask whether this particular Afghan can actually accomplish what he was bred to do."

She adds, "In defense of the judges, let me emphasize that they have to judge what comes in the ring that day. If the dogs are too bad, the judge can always withhold the ribbons or excuse them. But most of the time they're not that bad, so you have to judge what is in the ring. It's up to the breeder to breed a good dog.

"It is true that the judge can see a lot more from inside the ring than you can from outside the ring. Judging is a hard, thankless job," she adds. Adelene cites as an example one of her fellow judges, a nice looking man who always dresses well, carries himself well and is highly educated. She observes, "But when he judges, he frowns a lot." She recalls asking him when she first began judging why he frowned; he laughed and avoided giving an answer. After she had been a judge for a while, she told him that she finally understood his frowns. "Many times you are in the ring trying to find a dog that comes up to the standard and you can't find it. They're not bad enough to withhold a ribbon, but they're not all that good either."

Adelene feels that a good judge studies the breeds, has a good eye and goes in the ring to do his job. "He does not fiddle around putting on a show. He just does his job and goes right on with it."

Adelene firmly believes that a good judge evaluates the dog and does not look up at the other end of the lead to see who is handling. She also believes a good judge is not persuaded by magazine advertisements about certain dogs. "There are some very good dogs out there owned by people who don't have the money to advertise," she notes, adding, "You also have to learn to be very hard-shelled. It all goes back to the expression, 'To thine self be true.' When you're showing dogs, you can lie to everybody else, but you had better not lie to yourself about that dog on the end of the lead.

"A good handler can take a mediocre dog and make him look like a million dollars," she states, noting that an incompetent handler can "kill" or spoil the effect of a good dog. "If you work at it, then you're going to be good at it."

On many occasions Adelene has assisted novice handlers suffering from stage fright. "Sometimes a novice who is scared to death will come in with a very good dog. I can tell the person is scared to death; I like to talk them through it," she notes. "Normally I'll fix the collar for them and tell them to say 'pup pup pup' to get the dog going." She notes that if the dog is very good, even a person with stage fright won't detract from it. "You can see that the dog's good and you may have to talk them through it to keep them going. I've done it dozens of times."

Adelene is an honest judge who will not be intimidated by anyone. She recalls one experience when a handler attempted to intimidate her. "A handler came up to the ring, motioned me over and said, 'The major is in bitches.' He was implying that he expected me to pick his male for Winners Dog and Best of Winners so that he could have the major points.

"Well, Adelene Pardo will not be wired."

Adelene was worried about what she would do when the dogs came into the ring. She prayed that one of them would be better than that handler's dog. She adds, "A lady came in with a very nice puppy; my prayers were answered. She was scared to death, so I showed her how to put the lead on the throat and told her to say 'pup pup pup.' The puppy did really well, and I gave him

Winners Dog and Best of Winners." Adelene also reported the other handler's improper behavior to the AKC representative.

She recalls another incident that occurred in California as she was judging Labrador Retrievers. The ring steward indicated to her that a man standing near the judge's table had been staring at her. She replied, "Most likely he's trying to intimidate me, but I'll take care of him." She walked to the judge's book and pretended to be reading. "Then I brought my eyes up, and I looked right into his eyes as hard as I could. My students are familiar with those eyes when they do something wrong. He turned and walked away from the table." She notes, "He came back later that day with a special, came in the ring and showed his dog just as nice as could be with no trouble whatsoever." The ring steward said to Adelene, "If you looked at me like that I wouldn't give you any trouble either."

She adds, "I try to do everything right. I try to be honest. Most people, whether they like me or not, have a lot of respect for me." Mrs. Pardo is certified to judge all Sporting Group dogs, half of the breeds in the Hound Group, Junior Handling and Best in Show. She is constantly studying and attending seminars to expand her knowledge and expertise.

She concludes, "It's lots and lots of fun to judge a ring full of very good dogs. It makes your heart just sing. You can hear trumpets blowing when you see those beautiful dogs that are correct for their breed walk in the ring."

Mrs. Pardo's success as a judge is exemplified by the following letters:

Dear Mrs. Pardo,

I wanted to tell you thank you for being so nice to me on Sunday at the Polo grounds.

I was the one who had to take the place of the handler with a Golden bitch she was showing. The bitch doesn't even belong to me. I had never done anything like this before and had never taken a class either. I felt panicky, and you were wonderful to me. The poor dog was already a nervous wreck with the handler, but with your guidance, she and I both relaxed and started having fun. The handler did not give me any of her treats, and I had nothing to keep the bitch focused. I noticed that when you had me tell her "hup, hup, hup" as I was going away from you, she really perked up. I found myself forgetting about all the people outside of the ring; all I could think about was the dog. I had so much fun that I want to take classes and handle my own puppy from now on. Thank you again.

Sincerely,

Kathy Stevens

● ● ●

Dear Adelene:

I find myself in the delightful place of writing to thank you for the fabulous Group 1 you awarded to our "Rocky" in Mount Pleasant, Michigan this month. We've had a wonderful couple of months with Rocky, and this is now his 6th Group 1st.

It's truly a joy to have our dog win, but when you know that the judge is as tough as they come, expecting the most from the dog and the handler as a unit, well, the words "thrilling" and "proud" don't even come close. And when you know that the judge enjoys her work on that day and wants all the dogs in her ring to perform at their best, even urges them to do so, well, the words "excited" and "proud" don't even come close. And when you know that the judge has "been around the block" a few thousand times herself, and has "been there, done that," well, the words "overjoyed" and "proud" don't even come close!

Our hearts were pounding while we talked to each other on the telephone screaming, "He won the Group, he won, he won!" Thank you for your recognition of our dog and for giving us another memory to treasure in the years ahead.

With love,

Bill, Debbie and Dana

10

Today

I'm 70 years old, and I still train people to train their dogs, both in conformation and obedience. Lou came out of retirement and at 71, he drives a chemical tanker. When I go for my yearly checkup, one of my doctors always asks if I'm still in dogs. My answer to him is always, "'Til they slam the casket lid." I've always said about being in dogs, you can be in it until the day you die, because there are all kinds of work and things people can do, whether they're young and can run around the ring or whether they're old and just have to sit. There's still a lot of work to be done and a lot of people to be taught. Some people call me a matriarch, but I still look at myself as a kennel girl.

Adelene and Lou Pardo live on a large property near Alvin, Texas, with two retired champion male Weimaraners , Ch. W.C.'s Eye of the Tiger and Ch. Wynwood's Smoke Stack, and one female Lab-type rescue dog, Weimar Castle's My Name is Poo. Adelene has trained and will continue to train many champion dogs and handlers. In the tidy house filled with Weimaraner photographs and art, on her refrigerator is a poster, a gift from a student, that contains one of her favorite expressions:

Believe in the magic of your dreams.

*Adelene Cullum, age 14, on Tony,
one of Jim Lacina's horses,
in Yoakum, Texas.*

Adelene and Duchess, 1962.

Duchess, early 1960s.

Adelene's favorite photo of
Duchess, Ch. Duskin's Princess
Shellie, U.D., pointing birds.

*Adelene and Duchess,
Ch. Duskin's Princess Shellie,
U.D., winning first in Open B
Obedience, Oklahoma Kennel
Club, early 1960s.
Photo by Alexander.*

*Adelene and
Ch. W.C.'s
Thunderwheel
of Marquez,
C.D., 1965.*

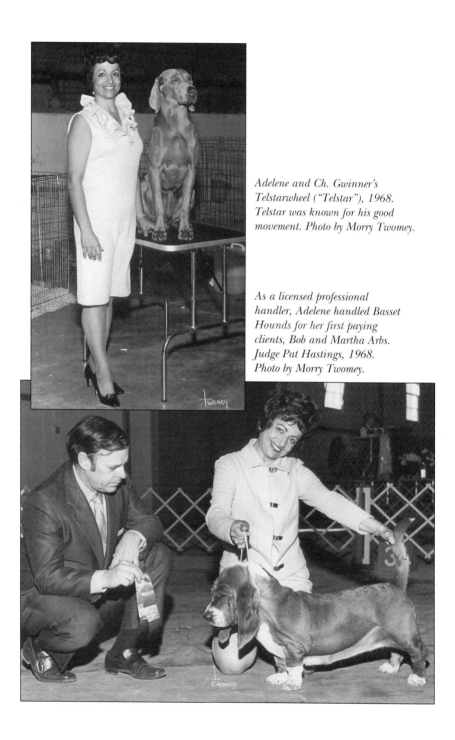

Adelene and Ch. Gwinner's Telstarwheel ("Telstar"), 1968. Telstar was known for his good movement. Photo by Morry Twomey.

As a licensed professional handler, Adelene handled Basset Hounds for her first paying clients, Bob and Martha Arbs. Judge Pat Hastings, 1968. Photo by Morry Twomey.

Ch. W.C.'s Johnnie Walker of Marsu winning Best of Winners under Judge Tom Rainey. Johnny Walker was a specialty winner. Early 1970s. Don Petrulis Photography.

Tony Gwinner and Ch. Lemans Flashing Silver Wheel ("Dusty") winning the Sporting Group in Lubbock, Texas, under Judge Frank Hayes Burch in 1971. Photo by Bill Francis.

Adelene and Spanky, Ch. Spanky of Our Gang, No. 1 American Staffordshire Terrier in the U.S., 1971. Photo by Sara Nugent, Spanky's owner.

Ch. Spanky of Our Gang ("Spanky") winning the Terrier Group, Dallas Kennel Club, Judge Roy Adair, 1971. Adelene handled Spanky to win the American Staffordshire Terrier National Specialty at the same show. Photo by Morry Twomey.

Lou Pardo
showing
Weimar Castle's
Let It Be Me
("Mimi")
under Judge
Tom Rainey.
Don Petrulis
Photography.

Lou Pardo and
Dorothy Nickles
clowning around
at a show in
Ft. Worth, Texas,
ca. 1972.
Photo by Bill
Francis.

Adelene moving Ch. Gwinner's Telstarwheel. Telstar was in the top 10 Weimars in the U.S. in 1968 and was known for his beautiful movement.

Mrs. Pardo insists the Borzoi was on a loose lead and she was merely nudging it with her finger in an attempt to achieve a better position in a small ring. Photo by Peggy Hemus.

Ch. W.C.'s The Dutchman of Dauntmar ("Dutchman") with Judge Joe Faegel and Adelene. This photo was taken the day the Dutchman hit the floor and Adelene stacked him back up in a matter of seconds, to the amusement of everyone around the ring except the judge, who didn't even notice. Photo by Morry Twomey.

*Dorothy Nickles
awarding Best in Show
to Adelene and W.C.'s
The Dutchman of
Dauntmar, San Jacinto
Kennel Club, April 1974.
Photo by Morry Twomey.*

*Adelene and the Dutchman
(Ch. W.C.'s The Dutchman of
Dauntmar) winning
Best in Show, 1974,
San Jacinto Kennel Club,
under Judge Dorothy Nickles*

Adelene and Ch. Weimar Castle's Mm! Mm! Good, 1976

Starwar (Ch. W.C.'s Starwarwheel of Ranah) winning Best of Breed with Judge Mrs. E. W. Tipton. New Orleans Kennel Club, 1979. J. D. Van Sickle Photography.

Adelene moving Dago (Ch. W.C.'s The Dynamic Dagowheel) on a loose lead in March 1979. Photo by Tom Pincus.

Adelene and Dago, Ch. W.C.'s The Dynamic Dagowheel. Photo by Tom Pincus.

Ch. W.C.'s The Dynamic Dagowheel won the Sporting Group at the Acadian Kennel Club show in 1978 under Judge Mrs. Huggins. Photo by Morry Twomey.

In 1987 Adelene judged Best in Show and awarded the prize to Shirlee Murray and her Irish Setter at the Arkansas kennel club. Don Petrulis Photography.

Adelene and Tiger Eye (Ch. W.C.'s Eye of the Tiger) as a puppy.

Adelene and Ch. W.C.'s Eye of the Tiger, 1994. Photo by Sheryl Stuchbery.

Ch. Wynwood's Smoke Stack winning Best of Breed under Judge Esme Treen at the Baytown Kennel Club show, 1995. Photo by Peggy Hemus.

11

What Is Loose-Lead Handling?

Years ago, one of the great handlers of the day showed a Whippet at Westminster. For Best in Show competition, he used a rescoe lead, but he pulled the slide clasp back so it had a big loop and it just lay on the dog's shoulders. That dog just gaited around and did his job with his head up. They won Best in Show that night; the commentator said, "And it couldn't have been a looser lead."

Adelene Pardo teaches the art of loose-lead conformation handling, believed by many to be the best possible way to show a dog because it allows more natural movement around the ring. There are many conformation showing techniques and theories advocated by countless experts, but "Adelene's way" of loose-lead handling is as successful today as it was 40 years ago. The following chapters present a framework for using loose-lead handling that will enable the reader to show his dog to its maximum potential.

A dog moving around the show ring on a loose lead presents a beautiful picture of fluid, balanced movement. Loose-lead handling utilizes a relaxed lead, with the collar or chain riding delicately on the dog's top neck bones, enabling the dog to move on his own center of gravity. A loose lead does not necessarily imply that the collar or chain is also loose. Successful loose-lead handling uses placement of the chain to communicate with the dog. That communication cannot be achieved if the chain is too loose or too tight.

One ring of the collar must be placed at the center of the dog's throat to enable the handler to be in touch with and control the dog. Through practice, the handler is able to balance the chain gently on the top of the dog's neck bones. Subtle corrections are communicated to the dog through the chain by tugging the lead and then relaxing it to its original position.

A dog pulled up very tightly by the chain and lead is unable to move around the ring in a natural, balanced gait. The "string-'em-up" technique of handling is commonly employed in the ring because that style does not require as much training. Mrs. Pardo contends that any dog can be trained to show on a loose lead, although some dispute this point. But she cautions that using a loose lead requires a certain amount of training for the dog and handler.

Many professional handlers agree that using a loose lead gives the dog a better appearance. But they also acknowledge that professional handlers don't normally have the time for training individual dogs that is available to owner-handlers. They point out that some dogs will move on a loose lead naturally and some will not. During her handling career, Adelene always took the time to train her dogs to show on a loose lead.

Mrs. Pardo began to learn loose-lead handling at her first dog show. She became acquainted with accomplished handlers early in her career and noticed that the most successful ones used a loose lead—or at least a partially loose lead—when moving dogs around the ring. She studied the more competitive and winning dogs and how the handlers moved them. She took copious notes and became skilled at correct use of the chain and lead. She learned that the dog should be noticed, not the handler. "Nothing should distract from the dog," she states. And she observes that a handler holding his dog on a tight lead, often struggling to hold him in place, distracts from the appearance of the dog.

A dog moving on a loose lead is not being pulled or tugged. Many handlers draw the dog's lead up tight, often pulling his feet off the floor and causing him to lose his balance. She offers the following examples: "If someone is helping you down the stairs they can take your arm and pull it up, and you are off balance. You'll fall instead of being able to walk down the stairs in a normal position. Similarly, when a child is learning to walk, an adult walking with the child will pull him up by the hand; the child cannot really balance because his feet just barely touch the ground. Holding a tight lead on a dog pulls him off-balance and affects his movement. And a dog's movement is the most important element in showing."

Any handling style should allow the dog to hold his head in the appropriate position required by the particular breed, but loose-lead handling also provides the handler with options should a correction be necessary. A gentle tug and then relaxation of the lead will communicate with the dog through the chain and remind him to hold his head as he has been trained. Due to varying bone structures and functions for which they were bred, different breeds of dogs carry their heads in distinct positions. For example, Terriers carry their heads higher than Sporting dogs. A Lhasa Apso or an Italian Greyhound will hold his head high. Border Collies should drop their heads level with their backs, but a Doberman carries his head high. Sporting dogs generally carry their heads a little above the withers. According to Adelene, any dog can be trained to hold his head in the proper position; a loose lead can be used to correct and facilitate the position of the head.

A common misconception about loose-lead handling is that the lead should be extremely loose. The lead should be relaxed just enough so the dog is flowing or moving easily and minor corrections can be achieved through quick tugs and releases of the lead.

After being trained, most dogs moving on a loose lead will try their best to do what the handler is asking of them. A well-bred dog will just naturally move according to his breed standard if he is well put together and handled in a way that enables correct movement. Adelene points out, however, that another key to successful showing is to start with a well-bred dog.

Adelene summarizes that the dog should move around the ring on a loose lead at all times, with the handler maintaining complete control through proper positioning and use of the choke chain. "An important point is training. A dog must be well trained to show successfully on a loose lead," she adds, concluding, "Training plus time, patience, and love are required to teach a dog to show on a loose lead."

12

Chains and Leads

A young boy in my class was showing a Pug, and
at the start of class he informed me that Pugs
are not shown on choke chains. I insisted that in my
class, he would train his dog on a choke chain and
move him on a loose lead. So the boy worked very hard
at it, but when he went to the shows, everyone told
him that he shouldn't use a choke chain on that Pug.
I always tell my students to disregard most people's
comments and to show their dogs as I've taught them.
I stand on my record; their dog will do well if they'll
just do as I tell them. This boy was in the ring. The last
time the dogs were to be moved around the ring, the
judge asked that they be moved on a loose lead. My
student was the only one in the ring who could control
his dog, make it move and show its stuff, on a loose
lead. He won the five-point major that day and
continued to win after that.

Correct positioning and use of the choke chain to communicate with the dog are fundamental to loose-lead handling. A handler who is unable to master precise placement and balance of the chain on the dog's neck or the sensitive touch required to communicate with and maneuver the dog through that chain will be unable to show a dog on a loose lead.

To place the choke chain correctly on the dog's neck, the chain is first pulled through the ring that is not connected to the lead. Next the chain, forming a circle, should be placed around the dog's neck so that the lead end is on top *(See Figure 1)*. The ring on the opposite end should be located under the dog's throat; the chain should be pulled comfortably tight *(See Figures 2 and 3)*. When the dog is moved on a loose lead, the chain will loosen slightly and ride behind the skull and ears, up and under the right ear, with the ring under the dog's throat *(See Figures 4 and 5)*. The dog takes subtle directions from the handler through

Figure 1

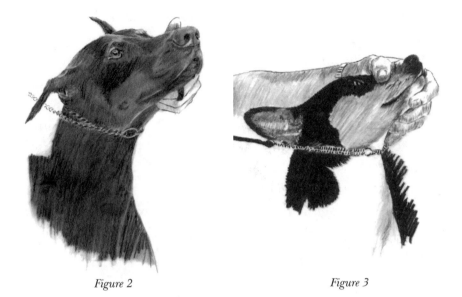

Figure 2   *Figure 3*

vibrations of the chain. Through practice, the handler will acquire a special touch that enables him to balance the chain on top of the dog's neck bones and leave some play in the lead.

Figure 4   *Figure 5*

A good quality choke chain and a narrow leather lead at least three feet long are crucial. The type and size of choke chain and lead are determined by the dog's size and breed. Adelene encourages use of a small link, but not too small. "Some choke chains look like a piece of thread, and you can't speak to the dog with a chain that small," she notes, adding, "The choke chain is used to communicate with your dog, just like the bit in a horse's mouth." Link size should be large enough to enable communication with the dog; larger breeds need larger links.

"If the dog lunges, he needs to be on a heavy choke chain and a heavy lead," Mrs. Pardo states. A dog that is difficult to handle may be initially trained with a larger link chain and then shown on a smaller chain. A well-trained dog may be shown on a leather or woven collar.

The chain or collar should be long enough to fit around the top of the dog's neck plus slightly more than a hand's width. The collar also should be long enough that, when pulled up and under the dog's throat, it is high enough off the head that the hand doesn't touch the dog's ears. The hands should not accidentally touch the ears, because this touch makes some dogs put the ears back and causes others to flick them around. The breeds that are required to hold their heads up very high with the neck arched can be trained by gentle corrections communicated through the ring under the throat. A choke chain that is too tight may cause the dog to twist his head.

A long lead enables the handler to back away from the dog when free-baiting him, so that the judge is better able to see the dog *(See Figure 6)*. A long lead also enables the handler to allow the dog to move out freely on his own to give the judge a better view. The lead should be at least three feet long, but it can be longer, depending upon the dog and the handler's abilities.

Figure 6

Adelene recommends a very narrow leather lead be used rather than nylon. "It is more difficult to control a dog on a nylon lead because it can be very slippery in the hands," she says.

Proper lead technique involves placing the "handle" or loop of the lead on the left thumb and taking up the lead backward and forward, accordion-fashion, until the lead has been taken up completely in the left hand. As the dog begins moving in the ring, the lead can be let out a little at a time. After the first two or three strides, the lead can be loosened a little until it is in the desired relaxed position. Mrs. Pardo states, "When a dog can flow on his own center of gravity, he will always look better. Bumping the dog or tightening the lead too much will interfere with the dog's movement and alter his appearance."

Movement

A woman who showed a winning Malamute came to me for handling lessons. She learned to move her dog on a very loose lead. The dog looked like he was moving slowly, but he wasn't. He was covering ground, but it wasn't obvious because he could move so well. He moved so easily that it looked like he was out for a Sunday afternoon stroll because she kept him on a loose lead. That's why they did so much winning.

"Movement of the dog is what separates the men from the boys in showing," Adelene states. She compares good movement to the dancing of Ginger Rogers and Fred Astaire. "When you set the collar so the ring is under the throat and you're moving your dog on a loose lead in whatever pattern, you want to look as if you're dancing together like Ginger Rogers and Fred Astaire," Adelene says. "When they danced together, they had a certain smoothness. They were two objects, but they looked like one. That's the way you want to be. You and your dog should move in unison."

Some may criticize this concept as theatrical. Adelene agrees, but she counters, "Anything that is pleasing to the eye will attract the human's attention. I always tell my students that they should float along like Fred and Ginger; they should move with some sparkle."

Good loose-lead movement is achieved by starting the dog off with the lead slightly tight. After the dog starts moving, the hand is dropped slightly, the lead is relaxed and the choke chain loosens up. "It really makes the dog look pretty," she says.

Adelene adds, "A good moving dog is not necessarily moving with a lot of speed. A dog that moves with ease merely creates the impression of speed."

Each breed moves around the ring at a different rate of speed. Individuals within the breed will move at different speeds. During training, the handler will sense a dog's correct speed. Good movement creates the appearance that the dog is covering ground. Adelene cautions, "Running fast and taking the dog around like you're in a race is not good movement. It's not correct movement. But if you put a dog on a loose lead and just let him ease along, he'll set the correct speed." The handler should not push the dog for too much speed. It is the handler's job to learn each dog's correct speed and how he looks his best. Some dogs need to be slowed down a bit, but that can be accomplished with training.

Some dogs may move out ahead of the handler, but the dog is steady, and the handler has taught the dog to move out. In this case, the dog may go out to the end of the lead, but he's not pulling the handler around. The lead is loose. If a handler chokes up on a dog when moving it, the dog may pound or hackney in front, or he may "elbow out." Many problems with the dog's front can appear if the lead is too tight. A dog moving correctly should have a topline so steady that an imaginary glass of water could be balanced on his back without spilling a drop.

Correct head position during movement can be achieved by using the ring under the throat. A gentle tug on the lead will press the ring against the throat and prompt the dog to hold his head where the handler indicates.

When moving around the ring, the dog should be positioned to the handler's left and slightly ahead, with its eyes and head forward. In obedience today, dogs are trained to watch the handler, stay close to him and look up into the handler's face. "If your dog is obedience-trained," Adelene cautions, "he will need to be re-trained for conformation." The dog in conformation must look straight ahead. "If the dog looks up at the handler, it can cause him to sidewind or sidetrack in his gait." Sidewinding is caused when a dog's front and rear ends are not properly aligned. "Also, some judges just don't like dogs looking up at the handlers," Adelene comments. "Different commands are necessary for conformation and obedience, and the attitude of training will have to be changed for the conformation ring." She encourages everyone to show in both disciplines. "It can be done; it just takes a lot of time, patience and love."

When moving a dog away from the judge, the good handler will glance back at the judge out of the corner of his eye to make sure the dog is traveling in a straight line away from the judge. Adelene recommends that the handler pick a person or object on a straight line from the judge to use as a guide. When handler and dog have moved across the ring and turned back toward the judge, a slight pause will allow the dog—especially a large breed —enough time to turn around the handler and return in a straight line toward the judge. Adelene compares this pause to a dance step.

After that slight pause, the handler moves the dog back again in a straight line toward the judge. It is important that the judge have the best possible view of the dog. Adelene says, "If both you and the dog do it with great class and ease of movement, you're going to get a longer look from the judge."

During the 10- or 15-minute daily training session, the handler should practice moving the dog at different speeds. Move him very slowly, then at a medium speed, finally at a faster speed. Then, the dog will take the command for whatever speed the judge indicates. Adelene instructs her students to use the command "easy" if the dog is moving too quickly. "Each time you say 'easy,' he'll slow down a little."

To practice gaiting with your dog, start off slowly and use the word "easy." If the dog lunges, give him a little correction and stop. Start over again, and say "easy," until he understands that you don't want him to pull against the lead. Mrs. Pardo notes, "Some dogs are very hyper; this is pretty common in Sporting dogs. Weimaraners will lunge to the end of the lead and want to pull the handler around. When this happens, just go in another direction, giving a little tug to the lead. When he gets back to you, go in another direction, and when he hits the end of the lead, give him a little correction. When you do it two or three times, he's finally going to understand what you want. Some dogs naturally pull ahead of the handler when moving around the ring. That's fine, but the dog must be well trained and very steady. If you let him go out in front of you too early, before he's trained, you won't have any control. But once the handler gets him under control, the dog can pull out ahead a little."

She continues, "Practice with your dog, and work hard so that everything comes naturally to you. How you hold the lead, the way the lead lies on the dog's neck, the way the lead comes off the neck and into your hand and up your arm, should all appear to be very natural." She suggests that the lead should continue in a line from the handler's shoulder down to the dog's neck. "Consider your shoulder and arm as part of the lead," she states. "You want to make it appear as if it's an everyday occurrence," she adds. "You should be able to do it without thinking, just like skating or riding a bicycle. You don't think about it after you've practiced and practiced, and it's the same with a dog."

Normally the judge is looking for breed type and movement. Adelene says, "I was always taught if a dog moves well, that means he's put together well." Some judges claim that they don't look at the way the dog is handled, but that is contrary to all the principles of good handling. "Good handling means making the dog look as good as possible," she states. The handler should be smooth and graceful and should never rush himself or the dog. The dog should be trained so that he moves nicely and easily at whatever speed is asked of him.

Adelene also advises the handler to talk to his dog while they are moving around the ring. "You've got to make him proud to be a part of the team. For example, you can say 'come on babe, come on, good boy, you're doing good, you're Mama's boy, that's a good boy, you're really moving, there you go, there you go.' If you talk to him—and you can say just about anything—he'll start listening and paying attention to you and not notice other things going on around him." Adelene says that when the handler and dog are in the ring, "There's no one in the world but you, the dog, and the person in the middle of the ring. No one else exists."

Ring Patterns

During a show many years ago in West Texas, a judge told a contestant, "I want you to make an 'L' pattern." An "L" pattern involves moving in a straight line away from the judge, turning left and moving across the end of the ring, then retracing the pattern to the original position. The woman moved away from the judge, across the end of the ring, and traced her steps back—with her little toy poodle tucked neatly under her arm.

Ring patterns, including movement, stacking and free-baiting, are determined by the preference of each judge. Every dog in the several classes of each breed is expected to be exhibited in the same pattern.

The most common pattern of movement requested by a judge is a diagonal across the ring. Some judges ask for different patterns, including a triangle, an "L," and very occasionally a "T." If the dog is trained to move at different speeds and the handler is in control, they should be able to execute any pattern. This training is essential.

In making the triangle pattern, handler and dog move away from the judge and down the right side of the ring. Then they turn left and move across to the other side of the ring, turn and come back toward the judge on a diagonal. When moving away and coming back to the judge, the dog, not the handler, should be in line with the judge to give him the best possible view of the dog's movement. A triangle pattern provides a rear view, a side view and the front view. When the judge instructs the handler to move all the way around the ring, he'll see another full view of the dog. The collar or chain should be carefully set before the dog begins moving; the handler should always have the lead adjusted and ready. A judge does not have time to wait for the handler who is fumbling with the collar or lead. Judges normally only have about two minutes to spend examining and watching each dog; every second is important.

When handler and dog are moving back toward the judge during execution of any pattern, they should stop about three feet from the judge; the handler should stand a little to the side so the judge can have a clear view of the dog. If the dog has an especially good front, it should be positioned with the front facing the judge. If the dog has a strong topline, it may be turned so the judge sees its profile. These positions set the dog up for free-baiting (See Figure 6, Chapter 12).

When making a pattern in front of the judge or going across the ring and back with a small dog like a Corgi, Dachshund, or Pomeranian, the handler should move around the dog. The judge's sight of the dog will not be broken if the handler steps around the dog. The best way is to step to the right, turning around in a small circle to the left, and the dog will also make a little U-turn. But the handler will make a bigger circle, so he must step to the right. Then the dog will start moving around. With this step to the right and a little tug to the collar, the lead will tighten up just a little and the dog will realize that he needs to make a U-turn when he sees the handler making a circle.

Stacking

I handled Basenjis for Nancy Pincus because of something that happened one day when she watched me show the Dutchman, one of my Weimaraners. He didn't like to show, and he would get crazy every now and then and act up. On this day, there was a loud noise; he dropped to the floor. I jerked him up quickly and got him back in a show stance. When the judge turned around and looked at me, I just grinned at him. Everyone around the ring started applauding, because I handled him so quickly, got him back in a show stance and even was able to smile at the judge. We won the Breed that day; Nancy Pincus said to her husband, Tom, "That's my handler."

A well-stacked, correctly proportioned dog of any breed is a beautiful sight. Dogs are stacked—placed in a show stance in the ring—at the judge's direction so that he may view and examine them. The handler positions the dog's head, feet, tail and body, and the dog is trained to hold that position during the judge's examination. Larger breeds are stacked on the ground; smaller breeds — "table dogs" — are stacked on a grooming table.

The first step in stacking a dog is to lift his head with the choke chain. The chain should be gently pulled up under the throat so that it runs around each side of the head directly under the ears and presses against the tonsils. If the dog needs correction, the chain can be pulled snugly against the tonsils. In this way, the dog's head can be controlled completely. "Control the head and you control the whole dog, just like with horses," Adelene notes. "Control the horse's head and you control the whole horse."

To set the front feet, hold the chain in the right hand, put the left hand over the dog and take the left elbow. Use the elbow to set the foot on the ground so that it is directly under the withers. Always use the elbow to move the front feet into position.

Change hands on the choke chain and use the right hand to position the right leg directly under the withers, using the dog's elbow to move his leg. The feet should be the same distance apart as the legs at the point where they connect to the body. The front legs should be straight up and down, perpendicular to the ground. After the front legs are placed, the chain can be set. Bringing the hand up and off the dog's neck so that the chain is no longer snug around the neck creates a frame for his head. Change hands on the chain again, and begin setting up the rear with the chain in the right hand.

Using the left hand, set the dog's left rear foot by catching the top of the hock joint and setting the hock, or flat part, of the leg perpendicular to the floor. Then set the right rear foot in the same manner. Some dogs need to have their feet pulled back a little farther to straighten the top line, but if the hock is vertical the rest of the body should come into place naturally. As a guide to correct positioning of the legs, imagine parallel lines drawn from the inside of the rear feet to the outside of the front feet *(See Figure 7).*

These three basic guidelines make setting up a dog's feet simple: position the front feet straight and under the withers; set the hocks vertical to the floor; and set the feet on a parallel line running from the inside of the rear feet to the outside of the front feet. Since each dog is a different width, some need to be set up with the legs wider apart than others. Some of the smaller breeds are set up with the rear legs not quite to the outside of the imaginary parallel lines.

By paying attention to the dog's body while he's being stacked, the

Figure 7

handler can detect whether the dog has moved his feet. Training is necessary to teach the dog to stand still and hold a stack. The commands "stand" and "stay" can be used during the stacking process. Adelene recommends putting the dog on a grooming table to teach him to stand very still. When the dog, large or small, is placed on a table, his feet can be positioned correctly and he can be taught to hold the stack. Adelene says, "As you're training a dog, always give him praise when he has done something right. Don't praise him when he's done something wrong. You want him to understand when you are pleased with what's going on between you."

For breeds that require the tail held up or extended level with the back, always make sure that the tail is held in a soft, gentle manner. Position your hand to have a light and pleasant look. Many dogs will hold their tails up on their own after sufficient training. Scratch the underside of the base of the tail, and say "tail" or "tail up," and the dog will learn to extend the tail and hold it up. "If you can teach a dog to shake hands, roll over and play dead, you can teach a dog to hold up its tail. You can even teach a dog that's frightened to hold up its tail," states Mrs. Pardo.

To better control the head during the stacking process, the fingers of the right hand may be placed under the jaw with the index finger in the "V" formed by the jaw bones. Pressing the index finger in the "V" gently toward the front or outward will keep the dog under control. When the dog begins responding, the pressure can be lessened. Another good technique for controlling a dog that is acting up involves using the thumb to press his lip against the canine tooth. "Do it gently, and if he starts behaving himself, it's fine. If he doesn't, press a little harder. This will give him the idea that there are things you can do to him when he's in the ring, because a lot of them get very ring-wise and think that you can't correct them or raise your voice in the ring," Adelene comments.

After the dog is stacked and the choke chain is pulled up in the right hand, the handler can place the index finger and thumb of his left hand just to the back of the withers, pressing straight down firmly, but not hard. "Just lay the fingers there," Adelene notes, adding, "If the dog starts to lean back, you can press a little harder and he will not lean back. It's almost like putting a dowel pin there; it will keep him from leaning back." Finding and using that pressure point will also keep the dog from leaning back during the examination or moving his head too much. Adelene reverts to her horse training knowledge for this tip, stating, "When you're riding a horse, especially in an English saddle, if you'll press your buttocks down, you can get the horse to do what you want because there's a pressure point. A dog has that same pressure point; it can be used very effectively to control his position. You do it with a lot of finesse." She continues, "Everything that you do—holding the lead, stacking the dog—has to be done with finesse so it will create that pretty picture you're working to achieve."

Placing the feet of a larger dog in the stack position may require extra care. When placing the left front foot using the dog's left elbow, use the choke chain to pull the dog slightly toward the opposite side. This will pull his weight off the left foot and make placement easier. The right foot can be placed in this same way by pulling the dog slightly to his left while using the right elbow to move the foot. Many of the large breed dogs don't like to have their feet lifted off the ground, so the rear feet may be slid back to the proper position. That will also keep the dog steadier and more balanced; the handler will have more control over him.

With some of the middle-sized and larger breeds, including Belgian Tervurens, Doberman Pinschers and Weimaraners, many handlers teach them to free stance and stand very still. When it's almost time for the judge to go over a dog, while he's moving the dog in front, the handler steps his dog up into a free stance. Just before the judge approaches him, the handler must have a firm grip on the dog's collar and must be in complete control of his dog when the judge starts to go over him. The dog should not be asked to stand in a free stance while he is being examined by the judge. The handler must be prepared for any incident that could possibly arise while the judge is examining the dog. The handler must be able to take control in a split second and should always try to make the judge feel comfortable around his dog, especially if it is a larger breed or a breed with a reputation for being a little aggressive. After the dog is stacked, the handler should watch the judge inconspicuously and try to present the dog to its best advantage.

When stacking a dog with a tendency to roach his back, rub the fingernails down into the coat on his back from the tail toward the head. "You're trying to create a sensation along the backbone that will cause him to straighten out his back," Adelene notes. "You'll sometimes find this roaching tendency in puppies and in dogs that are slightly timid."

Adelene cautions handlers, "When setting up your dog in a line of dogs in the ring, do not set your dog up too close to the one in front." She also notes that during ring movement, handlers should take care not to "run up" on the handler and dog in front, leaving no space in which to set up their own dogs. She adds, "I call it being a sheep. Don't be a sheep." When the handler is moving the dog, if he has taught the dog to move at the various speeds and will watch a couple of dogs ahead of him, he can anticipate when they're going to slow down. Adelene advises the handler to leave a good amount of space in front, and from the corner of his eye watch the handler behind. "When he starts to set up his dog, you can set your dog up in the middle of this space. I call it a frame of light. If the handler is jammed up against the dog in front and the dog behind is jammed up against him, his dog cannot be seen as well. This is especially true about dogs with long tails that have to be extended, like the Pointer, English Setter and Gordon Setter. Be sure to leave enough room so that the tail can be extended and not hit the dog or handler to the rear."

During her professional handling career, Adelene was famous for controlling the ring. She advises her students to adopt the same attitude. "You must take control of the ring. You must take control of your space. Remember, you have a place in that ring. It's all in how you use and control that space that makes you a good handler."

A nervous or uptight dog may come up too far on his pasterns. Adelene advises the handler in this situation to put the right hand under the jaw, take the choke chain in the left hand and gently bounce the dog, not taking its feet off the ground. She adds, "Just bouncing him a few times will relax him a little, and he'll stand on his front feet better when he's more relaxed."

Mrs. Pardo cautions that a dog's rear legs should not be pulled too far back in the stack position. Many handlers are in the habit of pulling their dogs too far back, breaking the line of the stifle and hock. Adelene notes, "It will make them look straight in the stifles and throw off the whole outline of the dog." She advises that placing the hock, or flat part of the back leg, straight up and down will cause the stifle to fall naturally into the correct position.

Some dogs also will lean forward over their fronts. In this situation, Adelene recommends the handler move around in front of the dog, place his hands on either side of the face and push him back gently. She says, "His feet will stay where they are, and the whole body will push back. If you do it two or three times, just real easy, he will learn that you don't want him to lean into his front."

A handler showing a large dog should always stay on his feet while the dog is stacked so he can look down over the dog and know that the feet are positioned correctly. Adelene suggests that if the handler with a large breed kneels, he can lose sight of important details regarding the dog's position.

She recommends some special exercises for a table dog if he is afraid or nervous and does not want to stand still. When practicing with the dog, the handler can simply pick him up and put him down quickly. "Just up and down quickly will kind of take the dog's breath away. He'll think he had better stand quietly or he will be moving up and down. Normally, you only have to do this a couple of times. When he's stood there a second or two, pat him on the chest and tell him OK. Then hug him, clap your hands and get all silly with him. Then put him back in a show stance. You should ask three or four people to walk around the table in a circle and reach out to stroke the dog on the back on the judge's side." Adelene recommends this technique to train the dog to be steady and hold the stack.

She cautions, "Remember, when you stack a dog, don't pull it toward you. You can make the dog's body twist if you pull it toward you, so always make sure you extend your arm so the dog's spine is in a straight line." With practice and Adelene's formula of "time, patience and love," the handler should feel comfortable stacking his dog and presenting that pretty picture to the judge.

16

That Winning Attitude

I always took my handling very seriously. I had a very good time with it, but I was very serious about it. Of course, I am one hell of a competitor. No matter what I do I'm going to be the best there is, whether I'm baking a cake or handling a dog.

Carolyn Willis recalls an example of Adelene's winning attitude while she was handling one of Carolyn's champion Malamutes, stating, "In those days, Malamutes did nothing in the Group competition. The podium where the pictures of Group winners were taken was in the center of the ring. In the Group competition, when the dogs were moved around for the judge the final time, my dog would just start pulling toward the podium to get on it. He knew he had won." The dog knew he had won because Adelene's self-confidence and triumphant attitude transferred down the lead to him.

Adelene's winning attitude is also illustrated by her advice to train the dog before he arrives at the show grounds. After training her dogs for months before a show, she would also work with them the night before at the show site. She would train with them and walk them around the show grounds to get them acclimated. She says, "I used to always laugh because the night before a show, I'd see people cooking steaks and having drinks. I'd be in the building training my dogs; they wondered why I won so much. They wondered why my dogs were so well-behaved in the ring. I was busy training them, walking them, playing with them, becoming buddies with them. I can have a steak and Coke any time I want."

Being very competitive came naturally to Adelene. "I was that way during World War II when we would sell bonds and defense stamps at school. I was in charge of selling defense stamps and always sold more than anyone else. I always work hard at being number one. There is no such thing as 'luck.' It's hard work. That's what luck is."

She notes that many people complain that some of the top handlers win over and over again. "But these top handlers are working, working, working. If they're not training their dogs, they're grooming them. One of the top handlers told me that Tuesday is toenail-cutting day; no matter what, they cut toenails every Tuesday to keep all the dogs in condition. They have beautifully groomed dogs because they work at it. They don't get that way by having a steak and drinking a Coke when they should be working, I guarantee."

Dog showing is a very competitive sport; the desire to win and the ability to work hard are basic elements of success. Adelene encourages her students to believe they are the very best. She says, "You've got to have a fire that burns deep in your gut to be a winner." She continues, "Your attitude is very important. If you have the attitude that you don't care what place you get, then stay home." She advises her students to work hard for first place and to be winners. "You won't win first every time, but 99 out of 100 times you'll win."

She stresses that training and showing a dog should be a serious endeavor. "You can have fun and laugh with your friends but you've got to be serious about the training. You can't be giggly. And your dog has to believe that you are serious. If you are not serious enough, you will never train a dog."

A good attitude is fundamental for successful dog showing. Adelene concludes, "You've got to want to win. You've got to want to breed good dogs." She adds that having a good dog to show is essential. "Many people try to finish a dog that is not necessarily a good example of his breed. Some of those can be finished when they're handled well, but it's better to start off with a good dog."

She concludes, "When you win, don't appear to be shocked that you won. Be proud of what you've done. Be proud of your dog. Be proud of the job that you two have done, say 'thank you, sir,' and go over to the first place. If you were that surprised to win, you ought to stay home because it implies that you feel your dog wasn't that good. Enjoy the moment! Enjoy the win!"

One of Mrs. Pardo's students gave her a refrigerator magnet containing the following:

> *Winners are everyday heroes. Winners take their dreams seriously. Winners never give up and won't let you give up either. Winners have attitude. Winners care in their sleep. Winners make big things happen a little at a time. Winners say "yes" to freedom and change. Winners go with the flow. Winners see the beginning in every ending. Winners expect the best. Winners inspire the best in others. Winners are the richest people in the world when it comes to experience, laughter and love.*
>
> —AUTHOR UNKNOWN

Dressing for the Ring

I laugh now about the dress I wore in my first dog show. It was a red tight-fitting dress that went a little past my knees with a big ruffle and net under it. I wore matching red wedge-heel shoes. Bob Ditmar, who raised cocker spaniels, was the ring steward; he told me, "The next time you go in the show ring, have on some tennis shoes. And don't wear a tight dress, just wear a nice suit with a skirt that comes to your knees."

The handler's appearance is a very important part of the picture he presents when showing a dog. "Nothing should distract from the dog," Adelene warns. A handler should look neat and clean and have on an attractive—but not necessarily expensive—suit of a color that compliments him and the dog. It's true that a dog show is not a style show, but Adelene firmly believes that the human eye is more naturally drawn to an attractive, neat handler and dog. She likes to point out that customers are usually more attracted to store employees who are neat and clean; she applies this same principle to proper showing attire.

Ladies should wear solid color suits that do not have long or flowing skirts. Pockets are mandatory. Adelene believes solid colors are best because prints, stripes and plaids may be a distraction. The skirt should be knee length and permit the handler to run. A skirt flowing and flopping at the ankles can slap the dog in the face and interfere with his movement or distract him, especially the smaller breeds.

The suit should be a pants suit or jacket and skirt. A pants suit should be a full pants suit; the jacket and pants should be the same color. The suit's color should contrast with the color of the dog. If the dog is black, the suit should not be black; the same principle applies to red or chocolate dogs. Khaki and brown colors may blend in too much with the dog's coloring. Adelene recommends bright, pretty colors that flatter the handler and contrast with the color of the dog. She comments, "After all, the handler is a backdrop for the dog, and it's the overall picture that counts."

Hair should be worn in a simple, neat style. Long hair should be pulled back tightly. Flying hair, scarves and ribbons are also potential distractions.

"In the complete picture, if you look nice with your dog and have on the right color, it's going to make your dog look good," she notes.

Men, of course, wear suits. But many of them wear brown so the dog hair won't be so obvious. Mrs. Pardo encourages men to wear brighter colored jackets that flatter them.

Shoes are another important part of the picture. Many handlers will show in white tennis shoes. But the flash of a white tennis shoe from across the ring can distract the judge's eye. Adelene stresses that a handler should always wear laced shoes of a color that does not distract the eye of the judge—brown, black or navy blue. Slip-on shoes may accidentally come off. She says, "The handler needs good-fitting, comfortable rubber-soled shoes that are good to run in and that tie on the foot, so that he doesn't waste any time worrying about falling down or losing a shoe." Sometimes the shows are held on slick floors with rubber mats. The dog has to stay on the mat or he may slip, and if it is a large dog, it can be difficult for the handler to also stay on the mat. Good footing is a must. As one of her former students jokes, "If you lose a shoe in the ring, Adelene will kill you!"

Adelene recalls an incident that occurred one year in Corpus Christi when she was showing an Elkhound. "Somehow, as we were moving around the ring, the dog got his right foot stuck in my right shoe. As my foot came forward, the shoe flipped up and hit the judge in the head. The judge asked, 'You do like to get a judge's attention, don't you?'" She concludes, "I have never figured out how it happened, unless it was mental telepathy, but it does illustrate my point about the importance of ring attire."

Adelene is a firm believer in removing as many uncertainties or variables as possible from the ring experience. Proper ring attire, including shoes that will not come off, is one element the handler is able to control. Confidence comes from knowing one is appropriately and practically dressed for any situation. Lack of that confidence may result in self-doubt and needless worry. If there is a possibility that a shoe may come off in the ring, worry can very easily become a truth. Merely thinking about falling can cause someone to fall. The handler will gain from not allowing himself to worry or show a lack of confidence because his dog can sense these feelings through the lead. Proper ring attire allows the handler to concentrate on showing his dog.

Time, Patience and Love

When you're starting to train your dog, give him a love name. Play a little game with this love name. I had a dog named "Dutchman," and I would call him "D-dog" and sing, "Come on, D-dog, come on, D-dog," just playing with him. Eventually I called him "Yee Yog," and I'd say "Come on, Yee Yog." I played a little game with him at home and then in the show ring. If he got a little down or got frightened, I would start playing with him using that love name.

M any people think they can train their dogs in a few minutes, but Adelene cautions that it takes "time, patience and love" to train a dog. Repetition is the key to training; as the dog improves, be sure to play with him after the training sessions so he will enjoy training. According to Adelene, "If the dog enjoys training, soon he's going to love it. He's going to become, as we call it in the dog world, a 'showing machine.' That's what you're working for."

Preparing a puppy to show involves training him well. He should learn to stack and move well. Adelene notes, "Many times, judges will not put puppies up because they're young. But if you have a good, well-trained puppy, that's the whole secret." If you have the attitude "I have the winner here," then you can win with the puppy. Adelene has proved that many times over by winning with her puppies. "It's just the attitude you put into it. But they must be trained. That is the secret word: training."

Training a puppy should always include a lot of fun. "Make a game of it," says Adelene. "Make the pup think he's the biggest thing walking. If you put a lot of fun into it, he'll stand there like royalty because it's fun and he knows that you're really enjoying it. Remember, a dog's whole life is to do what his master wants."

Adelene likes to start training puppies as soon as they can stand. When she was breeding Weimaraners and had a litter of puppies, she would put a grooming table next to the litter box, pick up the puppies one at a time and hold them up. They wouldn't even have their eyes open yet; she would let their feet dangle down and touch the table and say, "stand and stay." She would put the puppy up under her chin and say, "You're a good boy," because the dog can feel the vibrations and feel the hands touching him. By the time they opened their eyes and stood on all four feet, they could stand in a show stance. They knew what "stand and stay" meant from Adelene touching and holding them. "I only did it for a second or two," she adds.

When the pups are old enough to begin walking on lead, put on a heavy choke chain and heavy lead and let them walk around pulling them. "Give them a little yummy, love on them, pet them, talk to them, and let them follow you around. They'll get used to that lead and the clumsiness of it," she adds. "Then put on the little choke chain with a light leather lead with which you're going to show them, get an older dog and go out to your training spot. Put the older dog on the outside and the puppy next to you, then start walking." If the puppy is not cooperative, Adelene recommends using the phrase, "Come on, pup pup pup." She found that the words "pup pup pup" will get a puppy moving when nothing else will. Also, the puppy will go along with the older dog.

Adelene recommends teaching a puppy the "stand" and "stay" commands by putting him on a grooming table. "Put him up on the table; you don't really care where his feet are, you just want to teach him to stand still." If the puppy takes the "stand" and "stay" commands and stands for just a second, give him a little tap on the chest. When teaching him to stand and stay, use a tap on the chest and the "OK" command and he'll know that he can move. Adelene continues, "Clap your hands and talk baby talk and tell him how great he is. Then take him again and tell him to stand

and stay. If the puppy is very young, you don't need to place the feet in a show stance. You're just trying to get him to stand very still. And when he stands still, really praise him and get silly with him; make him understand that he's doing great."

As time goes on and the puppy is standing still, the legs may be placed in the correct positions. The back legs should not be pulled far back. Just place them slightly back, reinforcing the stand and stay. "If the puppy does not cooperate, pick him up real quickly in the air and then back down again to the table. It will take his breath away, and he will be more cooperative." Then when the dog stands still, praise him. Adelene says, "You can't give him enough praise and be silly enough with him when he has done something correctly. And don't praise him until he's done it correctly."

According to Adelene, a lot of people think they can't win points with puppies, but she states, "The way to win with a puppy is to have him trained like the older dogs. Then he'll walk into the ring like he's king. If he's a good dog in any breed and well-trained, he can win from the puppy classes. There are some judges that absolutely will not put up a puppy because they are afraid of what the dog will look like two or three years from that day. But when you're judging, it's that minute, that instant. That's how you judge the puppies." Many times during her professional handling career, Adelene heard judges say, "It goes to the puppy. He's trained."

She continued, "Don't wait to train your dog until you get to the point shows. Train him before you get there. Make it fun. Make him think he's the best, that he owns the world, that you and he together can whip anything. You should hug him, talk to him, and tell him how great he is. It takes time, patience and love. Don't forget this when you're training a dog. The dog must be trained to win but you don't have to make a mechanical object out of him. He should be happy. There's nothing more beautiful than a well-handled, well-trained dog that loves showing and is part of your life." Many would-be dog exhibitors are discouraged when they realize the amount of time they need to put into training their dogs. "One student at her third obedience lesson asked me about entering competitions. Her dog could not even heel and she thought they were ready for the obedience ring," she laughs.

"You can fire up a dog and get him happy with that love name. Sometimes when it gets down to the nitty-gritty, and a judge is trying to decide between your dog and another dog, maybe your dog is getting a little tired. If you'll talk to him with that love name, that will fire him up a little and make him go that extra little step that you need to really show your dog."

When training a dog, the handler needs to be firm with corrections in order to make the dog understand what he is being commanded—not asked—to do. If the dog is not following a command, it's because the handler is not communicating with him. Adelene adds, "You've also got to play with him. You've got to make him understand how happy you are that he's working so hard and that he's such a great dog. You've got to give him lots of love. It's time, patience and love."

Adelene likes to prepare her dogs for as many possibilities as she can imagine. "Stack the dog, then have the people with whom you practice pet him very firmly on both sides and on his hips, and make the dog hold the stack. When your dog comes up against a judge with very hard or firm hands, he will not be uncomfortable because you have trained him for this possibility." She adds, "Always praise the dog after he's stood for the guy with the greasy hands or the person who's petting him very firmly."

She says that a dog learning to stack or stand-stay should be trained in different locations. The same principle applies to a table dog. Adelene notes, "If you see a wall, put him next to the wall and stack him." Training around distracting noises is another good idea. "Let a tennis shoe tumble around in the dryer, then stack the dog. Just keep talking and making him understand that he must stand there, and he'll stand. He'll get used to anything. Then if there is a lot of noise or dogs fighting at a dog show, for example, your dog will be very steady. You always want a steady dog so that you and he can take control in any situation. You and the dog will be partners."

Adelene also suggests creating scent distractions for training purposes. "Dogs don't like the smell of gasoline, grease and oil. I used to visit my mechanic friends at their shops. I would stack the dogs and let the mechanics pet them with that oil and grease smell on their hands. The dogs get accustomed to it."

When you tell a dog to "stand" and "stay" and he starts to move, say "no." He will learn that the word "no" means to cease what he's doing. The dog may be fence fighting or trying to get a cookie off the cabinet. The word "no" is very important because it teaches the dog to quit doing what he's doing. Adelene notes, "There is no such command as 'uh.' A lot of people will say, 'Uh-uh-uh.' There's no such command. Say, 'No.' That means, 'You've done something wrong.' If he's moved, 'No' means, 'Don't do it.' Say, 'No. Stand.' That means, 'No, you were not supposed to move, stand is what you're supposed to be doing.' Then put him back into his show stance, placing the feet back into position."

Adelene uses her own dogs as an example of her training philosophy. "I tell everyone about my Weimaraners. They are the most spoiled brats that ever existed. My chiropractor's wife calls my dogs 'spoiled, rich brats.'" She adds, "They have all the toys they want, they get to lie on the bed, they have the best of food. But when I tell them to down, sit, come and stay, they do it because I have given them the command." Adelene concludes that she teaches people to train their dogs in much the same way as her mother trained her. "She only spoke to me once. And I loved her dearly."

19

Baiting the Dog

We worked with Tony and Gabby Gwinner for many years. He paid for our meals and lodging but said he wished he had just paid a salary because I was always eating. One year on the New Mexico circuit, I was grooming and eating away at a big bag of M&Ms. Late in the day about Group time, Tony asked about the bag of M&Ms. I couldn't tell him I had eaten the whole bag of candy, so I said I didn't know where it was. It turned out he used them as bait for his Chow-Chow. I never could bring myself to tell him what happened to his M&Ms.

Adelene uses this story to illustrate the concept that the handler should experiment to find the best bait for each dog. Some dogs, known as "chow hounds," will show their best for any kind of bait, while others are very particular. Adelene highly recommends liver, stating, "Liver is a very good bait because it fires up the dogs yet makes them stand staunchly at attention." And she adds, "Bait only after you have come back to the judge at the end of a pattern or if you're in a big class. Do not let it appear as if you are feeding the dog."

Adelene's recipe for cooking liver is very simple. "Buy a pound or two of the cheapest beef or pork liver available. Chicken liver is not good because it is too soft after it's cooked. Leave the pieces the original size. Put the liver in a pot and fill with water to cover about an inch. Spice it up with green pepper, salt, pepper, garlic, onions, celery or just about anything to make a nice taste." Adelene compares making liver to cooking a good pot roast. "Boil the liver slowly for 35 or 40 minutes. Pour it into the sink, wash it off and spread the pieces on cookie sheets. Bake the liver for ten or fifteen minutes at 350 degrees." Adelene suggests storing the large pieces of liver in the freezer in plastic bags or containers until needed.

She notes that liver should be kept as cold and dry as possible when it is transported to a show.

Cautioning all handlers to watch their dogs carefully as they are preparing the bait, she recalls an incident from her show career. "I cooked two pounds of liver to take to the shows and poured it into the sink. I asked my father to wipe it off and put it in plastic bags while I packed the motor home. Dago, who loved to eat, was in the house." She returned to the kitchen to find that Dago had eaten all the liver when her father wasn't looking. "Not only did I have to worry about the side-effects of all that liver in Dago's stomach, I had to buy more liver from one of the show vendors because there was no time to make another batch."

According to Adelene, a large piece of liver should be taken into the ring and smaller pieces may be broken off as needed. A large piece of liver is much easier for the handler to manipulate and much easier for the dog to see and smell. Some dogs will bait off the smell, while other dogs want to see the liver.

Adelene recalls, "When my mother wanted us to eat carrots and vegetables that we didn't like, she would make a coconut cake. She'd set it on the counter and tell us that if we ate our carrots, we could have some cake. So we'd eat our carrots; then we got a piece of coconut cake." She remembers one special time her mother cooked carrots and other vegetables and told her family to eat them. "Of course, we were thinking we would get some cake. Well, she didn't have a coconut cake that night. So from then on, she had to show us the coconut cake before we ate the carrots." She uses that story to demonstrate how some dogs need to see the bait. She concludes, "They are thinking, 'I'm not looking at you unless I can see the liver.'"

She notes that grilled chicken is also a popular bait, as are the processed rolls of bait sold mainly at dog shows. She jokes that one of her students, who is a professional handler, once carried what looked like a deli selection to the shows. She would open her cooler to reveal several different kinds of bait, all neatly packed in separate compartments.

For Adelene, excessive use of bait in the ring implies that the handler does not have his dog well trained and has to control it with food. She points out, "One day you'll walk in and the judge will forbid bait in his ring. Then you're going to be in trouble. But if you have a well-trained dog, you won't have anything to worry about." Adelene adds, "When you sit ringside and watch people show their dogs, you'll see the difference between the good handlers who don't bait the dog to make him stand and the others stuffing liver down his throat."

On a recent judging assignment in Phoenix, if someone was baiting a dog too much, she asked them not to bait the dog while she was going over it. One of the handlers asked, "How do you expect me to get the dog to stand still?" She replied, "Did you ever think of training it?" He said, "You know, you've got a good point."

She continues, "During the movement, I noticed one handler who would touch the dog on the nose with the liver about every fourth step. Of course the dog was jumping up on her; he liked the liver so he was trying to get it. When she got back around to me, I asked her to give me the liver and move the dog again; the dog went around the ring just fine without the liver." Mrs. Pardo notes that a small bit of baiting on the return to the judge is acceptable, or in a large class of 12 or 15, it is permissible to play with the dog and bait him. She adds, "The judges dislike excessive baiting and they talk about it. They really don't want it done."

Adelene cautions the handler not to flash bait in the air in front of the dog when beginning to move around the ring. "A dog should move in a nice, easy movement because you've told him to, not because he's running after a piece of liver."

She continues, "There are many breeds where the head is very important. The standard will stress the head, the way the ears are set, the way the neck comes out of the shoulders, whether the ears should be straight up or forward. Excessive baiting can obstruct the judge's view of the dog's head and distort the dog's position. Bad posture can be a result of pushing bait down the dog's throat with the nose straight up in the air, causing the dog's head and neck to sink into the shoulders. If the head and arch of the neck are so important, they should not be obscured by the handler's body or hand. The handler should back away from the dog. The dog should be taught to stand with his neck arched. The place to train the dog is at home, not when you've paid $25 for an entry fee and driven 300 miles to get to the show."

One technique for baiting a dog is to back away from him 3 or 4 feet, and when he's standing still, roll the bait around in the fingers. When the dog is under control, the handler will be able to step back from him. The height at which the bait is held varies according to the dog's size. With Dachshunds or Beagles and the smaller breeds, the hands should be about knee-high. With larger dogs like Setters or Retrievers, the bait should be about waist-high. Rolling the bait in the fingers or hands will cause the dog to search it out; as a result, the dog will have a more interesting expression on his face and in his eyes.

Another technique involves letting the dog smell the bait and then tossing it five or six feet away with your right hand. The dog will watch it and arch his neck as he sees it slide out across the floor. "One time, I was showing in Ann Rogers Clark's ring. She had me go down and back and as I came up to her, I had the liver ready and threw it. I meant for it to go out of the ring, but it hit her. Of course, I was as embarrassed as you can get. But she was a good sport about it," she recalls. Adelene stresses, however, that most judges are not amused if they are hit with flying bait.

Adelene cautions that the dog should not get a bite or reward while the judge is watching. "After the judge sends you around and you are back in line, then give your dog a little bite. Or if you are waiting in a big class of maybe 12 or 14, you can put the dog in a show stance and back away from him, then step forward and give him the liver. That way the dog knows that you're going to bring the liver to him; he won't be stepping up to you. He'll learn to hold his show stance and wait for the bait." To signal the dog to break the stance, open the hand palm up, slap him lightly on the chest and say, "OK."

At feeding time, the food bowl may be used to teach the "wait" command for free-baiting. Before giving the dog dinner, show him the food bowl and let him smell it. Use the "wait" command and let him stand just a minute looking at the food. If he doesn't wait, don't give him the food. Try the exercise later and don't give him dinner until he waits properly. In this way the dog will learn that if he waits, the food will come to him.

After learning the "wait" command, when handler and dog are moving back toward the judge, the dog will stop and look up if he hears the "wait" command because he's looking for the food. The word "wait" will mean food to him if this command is used every time he is fed. He does not need to be in a show stance during this pause as long as he's standing very still, looking at the food bowl. The "wait" command will help the handler gain more control over the dog.

Adelene notes, "When you see a handler feeding a dog rather than baiting him, it means that the handler cannot control the dog or has not trained it. He has to use bait to keep the dog still.

With time, patience and love, you can teach a dog to stand and stay."

Another free-baiting tip is to place the dog on a table, show the bait and stand out away from him. A grooming table, or any similar table, is suitable for this exercise. A small dog will be careful to stand very still and not to fall off the table. If the dog is a young large breed, he can also be taught to stand very still on a table.

"The most important aspect is that the handler and dog learn to be partners. A dog does not respect the handler who feeds him all the time, and the handler is not respecting the dog. It's like a feeding frenzy," she states. Mrs. Pardo notes that too often when she is judging, she looks down the line of dogs and sees this feeding frenzy. "I've even had handlers, when I start to look at the teeth, give the dog a nice big piece of liver. Many dogs love to eat; if anyone tries to get food out of their mouths, they will bite. You don't want that happening to the judge because you will be disqualified."

In summary, Mrs. Pardo encourages the handler to seek out his dog's favorite bait, train with it carefully and use bait wisely and judiciously to show his dog in the best possible way.

At the Show

When you go in the ring, if you get beat, you've got to come out with your head up high. Remember, your dog went in a great dog; he's going to walk out a great dog, win, lose or draw. I know it's not easy to lose. Many a time when I'd lose I'd go back to the motor home and knock holes in the crates inside, but I never did show it in front of anyone. You always want to leave the ring with great dignity.

Dog owners, handlers and breeders have been exhibiting dogs for over a century for the chief purpose of improving their breeding stock. The dog show fancy has grown over the years into a popular sport that combines the spirit of competition with the joy of seeing beautiful dogs.

The American Kennel Club, founded in 1884 to promote study, breeding and exhibiting of purebred dogs, governs and maintains official records for over 13,000 sanctioned dog shows each year. The AKC is a parent club for local and national breed clubs. Other national kennel clubs include United Kennel Club, World Kennel Club and Continental Kennel Club.

Conformation showing, the most popular dog show event, is based on a dog's overall appearance and structure. Other events, many of which are rapidly growing in popularity, include obedience, agility and events of instinct and trainability, such as field trials or herding tests.

In AKC conformation showing, professional and amateur handlers present dogs to judges, who examine and compare them with a mental image of the perfect dog that is based on a standard established by the national breed club and approved by the AKC. The judging process begins with males of each breed shown in various classes (puppies six to nine months, puppies nine to 12 months, puppies 12 to 18 months, American-bred, bred-by-exhibitor and open). Winners Dog and Reserve Winners Dog are selected from all first-place class winners. In certain breeds, the various classes may also be divided by color. Next the same classes of females are exhibited, and the judge selects Winners Bitch and Reserve Winners Bitch. Winners Dog and Winners Bitch then compete with the champions of record in the "breed ring" for Best of Breed. Best Opposite Sex and Best of Winners are also chosen. Best of Breed winners then move to Group competitions. The seven Groups are Sporting, Hounds, Working, Terrier, Toy, Non-Sporting and Herding. Group placements of 1 through 4 are made, and all Group 1 winners from the seven Groups then compete for Best in Show.

From one to five points are awarded to Winners Dog and Winners Bitch, depending upon the number of entries shown in each sex and breed. When a dog accumulates 15 points, including two majors (wins of three, four or five points), under at least two different judges, he has earned the title of AKC "Champion of Record," and the letters "Ch." are placed before his name. All Champions are eligible to compete for Best of Breed at any show without entering the class competition.

A point scale is published at the end of the show catalog breed listing that specifies the number of dogs and bitches required for the various points from one through five. The number of dogs and bitches shown—not merely entered—in the different classes including puppy, novice, American-bred, 12 to 18 months, bred-by-exhibitor and open, will determine the points awarded that day for Winners Dog and Winners Bitch. When the Champions or specials go in, the dogs and bitches are judged against each other for Best of Breed, Best Opposite and Best of Winners. If Winners Dog wins Best of Winners, for example, and if there's a major in bitches, the dog picks up her points. Winners Bitch doesn't lose her points, but Winners Dog will win the same number of points.

Adelene advises all exhibitors to check the tear sheets from the judges' book at the superintendent's desk to determine whether a show is a major in each breed. She warns, "Don't trust anyone to tell you whether the dogs are absent. Always look at those tear sheets. Many times people take the word of others and find it's not the correct number."

Mrs. Pardo stresses the importance of good sportsmanship in the sport of dog showing. She notes, "I used to call out to the person and then point, to let them know I was acknowledging that they had won. I would say we won more than we lost, but you should always have good sportsmanship. There are times when you know that you have been nailed to the wall, but you just have to attribute it to the people you're dealing with and go on showing your dog and being a good sport."

Sandra League, a top professional handler and student of Mrs. Pardo, traveled with her as a handling assistant for about 10 years starting at age eight. She states, "She taught me how to win as well as lose and to always hold my head up high and respect everyone. It was Mrs. Pardo's training and guidance that allowed me to continue handling dogs for over 30 years."

Ms. League recounts an incident from her days as a junior handler: "One time in Junior Showmanship I won my class, but I didn't win best Junior Handler. I was probably 10 years old. I threw a fit, pouted, ran to the motor home and got on the top bunk. Mrs. Pardo pulled me out and said 'Get down, get back in the building and hold your head up now!'"

Good sportsmanship should also be demonstrated toward kennel club members and volunteers working at the show. Adelene cautions, "When you're showing dogs, always be very nice to the ring stewards. Ring stewarding is a very difficult job done by volunteers. When the steward tells you how he wants you in the ring, remember that it's not his idea. The judge has told him how he wants the dogs brought in. Don't get testy with the ring stewards, because it may come back to haunt you some day." She also recommends picking up the armband from the ring steward shortly before the class begins and asking the steward for it by number.

All exhibitors should obtain the appropriate breed standard from the AKC and learn it. "Many exhibitors don't know the standard of their own breed," notes Adelene. She adds that it is necessary to start out with a good dog that is correct according to the breed standard. "Sometimes people want me to show them how to use handling to hide their dogs' faults. If you're covering up these faults and you're winning with a dog, how are you going to breed it? You want a good dog. You want to breed good dogs. You should not finish a dog just to be finishing him. Remember that all these puppies are going to be breeding stock one day." She concludes, "You have to have a good dog, he should be well-trained and it's all in how you work together."

Adelene advises, "After you've won and you're taking the picture with your dog, don't rush it. Make sure you have the dog well stacked. The photographer, if he's good, will assist you with positioning." She continues, "Many times, people are so thrilled that they've won that they forget about making a good picture. You always want to have a good picture, so take time to set the dog up properly."

Special care and consideration should be taken in showing a dog's mouth to the judge. The most graceful way to open the dog's mouth is to place the right hand under the jaw and use the left hand to pull up the lips. Make sure that the judge has a full view of the teeth. Be very relaxed and free when showing the teeth to the judge and try not to let the hands obscure the judge's view. Use the fingertips to pull the top and bottom lips apart. If the judge requests, show both sides of the mouth. Some standards contain requirements concerning missing teeth so the judge will, from time to time, examine both sides of the mouth. Some judges will count each tooth.

Adelene suggests an exercise for the dog who balks at having his teeth examined. "When your dog is at home walking around the house and he passes you, just take his head, open the mouth and look at the teeth, then give him a pat or hug. This kind of casual exercise, repeated several times a day, will give the dog a more relaxed attitude about having his teeth examined in the ring. Even a dog who does not like to surrender control of his head will learn that he should stand very still and let you look at or show the teeth."

On the show grounds, metal, wooden or plastic crates should always be placed in well-ventilated locations in the crated area. Adelene notes, "When I walk around the grooming area of a show, I see too many dogs lying in wire crates with people dripping cokes and coffee on them through the wires." She advises exhibitors to cover at least the back and sides of the crate with a sheet so the dog can have a little privacy and be more protected. She adds, "He'll rest a lot better; you'll get a lot more out of him when you start to show him. So many people forget that, although dogs have more stamina than humans, they get tired just like we do." She notes that dogs crated overnight in a show venue don't really get rest at night because they hear every little noise. "They really sleep in just a twilight sleep. They don't get into a heavy sleep, because of the noises around them in a strange place. Always remember your pup and be considerate in how you crate him."

Mrs. Pardo recommends a certain amount of control be exerted when dogs are being walked on flex leads—across a show site parking lot, for example. She states, "Make them stay back with you, so they're not tripping people or running up to other dogs. When you're ready for them to move away from you, pat them on the side and say, 'OK.' The OK signals that they can run on out and exercise. You must have control of your dog. At a show, dogs should not be permitted to nose each other because of the possibility of fights. The dogs may act friendly at first. You may know what your dog is going to do, but you cannot know what the other dog may do. Always have good manners and be considerate of other people and their dogs."

Perhaps the most precious gift that results from training for any event is the bond that develops between man and his animal. A close bond between dog and handler is another key to success in the show ring. Adelene recommends frequent petting and hugging be incorporated into daily life. "When he breathes, you breathe," she adds, continuing, "When your heart beats, his heart beats. You want to be a team. You want to be pals. You want to be showmen." She continues, "Let him know he's a special part of your life, because when you get in the ring, that bonding will be a plus. The more the dog loves you, the harder he'll work."

She recalls that Tony Gwinner would give each dog in his "string" a ball of hamburger meat every day. "He called all of them 'Buddy.' I can hear him now saying, 'Hi, Buddy.' He'd pet and hug them, and that's how he got close to them." Forming a bond with the dog makes for easier training and easier showing.

Show Your Dog!

A woman remarked at ringside after watching one of my students, "That girl in the blue suit certainly moves her dog well on a nice loose lead, at a nice pace." My student and her dog had a beautiful look; that woman's eye went right to them. That's what your work should accomplish!

That "beautiful picture" Adelene encourages her students to create in the ring encompasses many factors. The primary detail is good movement, which is achieved by allowing the dog to move freely and naturally on a loose lead, with the handler matching his pace in a smooth, graceful, and controlled manner. Adelene uses Fred Astaire and Ginger Rogers as an example and advises her students to dance as a unit with their dogs.

Correct positioning and use of the choke chain to control the dog is essential to good movement. If the handler is unable to develop the fine touch required to balance the choke chain on the dog's top neck bones with the ring under his throat, he will not be able to maintain control of the dog to allow for that free, natural movement.

A handler moving a dog on a controlled, yet loose, lead should practice every pattern at every speed and be able to execute any pattern of movement the judge requests. Training and experience will give the handler the flexibility to follow the judge's directions.

The three criteria for stacking a dog cannot be emphasized too often: (1) position the front feet perpendicular to the floor and directly under the withers, (2) set the hocks vertical to the floor and (3) place the front and rear feet according to imaginary parallel lines running from the inside of the rear feet to the outside of the front feet. Remembering these points in the ring can simplify the stacking process and result in a neat, clean stack or show stance.

A winning attitude is important because not only is the handler "selling" his dog to the judge, the dog is able to sense the handler's state of mind. A positive attitude that radiates confidence and the desire to win is fundamental for success in the show ring.

Proper ring attire may seem unimportant; however, dressing in a manner that shows the dog at his best while eliminating worry or insecurity is simply good common sense. Well thought-out attire is an important contribution to that pretty picture.

Adelene is an advocate of frequent and short, but positive, training sessions. The trainer or handler should make training fun for the dog so that it loves to show. The result will be "a showing machine" created using "time, patience and love."

Excessive baiting of the dog can be a distraction for the judge, can spoil the look of the dog and may reveal a lack of training. Mrs. Pardo encourages judicious and careful use of the bait in a more subtle manner than what is commonly seen in the show ring.

Adelene stresses good sportsmanship, win or lose, and advises her students to leave the ring with great dignity, no matter what the results. The dog should always be treated as a winner.

A combination of these components can result in a confident, relaxed handler showing his dog to its maximum potential, thereby presenting that beautiful picture to the judge. As Adelene would say, "Do your job, and show your dog!"